Destination: Holy Land

Destination: Holy Land

My Bucket List Journey with Jesus

BOB CYPHERS

RESOURCE *Publications* • Eugene, Oregon

DESTINATION: HOLY LAND
My Bucket List Journey with Jesus

Copyright © 2025 Bob Cyphers. All rights reserved. Except for brief quotations in critical publications or reviews, no part of this book may be reproduced in any manner without prior written permission from the publisher. Write: Permissions, Wipf and Stock Publishers, 199 W. 8th Ave., Suite 3, Eugene, OR 97401.

Resource Publications
An Imprint of Wipf and Stock Publishers
199 W. 8th Ave., Suite 3
Eugene, OR 97401

www.wipfandstock.com

PAPERBACK ISBN: 979-8-3852-3876-7
HARDCOVER ISBN: 979-8-3852-3877-4
EBOOK ISBN: 979-8-3852-3878-1

To my children, Christian, Austin and Dylan. May your heart beat in faith like your fathers. And to my grandchildren, Noah, Amira and Turner. May someday you walk where your grandfather walked, in the path of Jesus.

Contents

ACKNOWLEDGEMENTS ix
INTRO xi
CHAPTER 1 O'Hare 1
CHAPTER 2 Haifa 6
CHAPTER 3 Elijah's Cave 12
CHAPTER 4 The Wailing Wall 16
CHAPTER 5 Beit Sahour 21
CHAPTER 6 The Church of Annunciation 26
CHAPTER 7 Ein Karem-Church of the Visitation 31
CHAPTER 8 Bethlehem 36
CHAPTER 9 The Shepherds' Field 41
CHAPTER 10 Basilica of the Nativity 46
CHAPTER 11 Milk Grotto 51
CHAPTER 12 Nazareth 56
CHAPTER 13 The Jordan River 61
CHAPTER 14 The Mount of Temptation 66
CHAPTER 15 The Sea of Galilee 71
CHAPTER 16 Cana 76
CHAPTER 17 The Church of St. Anne 81
CHAPTER 18 The Mount of Beatitudes 87
CHAPTER 19 Magdala 92
CHAPTER 20 Mount Tabor 97
CHAPTER 21 Capernaum 102
CHAPTER 22 Bethany 107

Contents

CHAPTER 23 The Temple of Pan 112
CHAPTER 24 Tabgha 117
CHAPTER 25 Jerusalem 122
CHAPTER 26 The Churches 127
CHAPTER 27 The Last Supper 132
CHAPTER 28 The Grotto of Gethsemane 137
CHAPTER 29 The Garden of Gethsemane 142
CHAPTER 30 Gallicantu 147
CHAPTER 31 The Way of the Cross 152
CHAPTER 32 The Holy Sepulcher 157
CHAPTER 33 Ascension Chapel 162
CHAPTER 34 The Road to Emmaus 167
CHAPTER 35 Ben Guiron 172
AMEN 176

ACKNOWLEDGEMENTS

To Gretta Couri, who made this trip possible for me. And to her husband Gene, who never dropped his camera. I am in awe of both of your faiths. And to my wife Alison, who wrote every word with me, encouraging me to keep telling my story for others to hear.

INTRO

My bucket list only had one item: the Holy Land. Nothing else could possibly compare. And when I finally had the chance to visit Bethlehem, and kneel at the manger site, and then to visit Capernaum, and walk in the Sea Of Galilee, and then Jerusalem, where I prayed in the Garden of Gethsemane and carried the cross to Calvary … it is hard to even describe. Putting it into words that can take the reader on the journey with me, seeing what I see, feeling what I feel? A real challenge. For me to relive the visit, one step at a time? Exhilarating.

And then I sat down to begin writing, turned on the television, and watched in horror as the bombs began dropping on Israel. What I saw then, and what I saw now, were two different worlds.

CHAPTER I

O'Hare

"There are seven days in a week and someday isn't one of them."

At 65 years old, it was time for my someday.

The journey began with a bus ride from Peoria, Illinois to O'Hare airport in Chicago. There I would meet the other people I would be closely traveling with, a large group sharing the last name Couri, a family from central Illinois. Gene and Gretta, Tony and Marybeth, Aggie, and Ilda. Also in the group were Diana Joseph, Lolly Maroon, and Delores Koury.

"The one with a K," she proudly told everyone.

As we walked to our gate, reality set in.

"Last chance for a Mountain Dew, Bob," Ilda Couri said, smiling at me.

She was not aware that I had packed well. Very well.

We arrived at our gate and I looked out the window at the United Dreamliner that awaited me. The journey of my lifetime had arrived. Nightfall was setting in. Fourteen hours in the air in a cramped chair would be time for reflection of my faith. I paused and gave thanks for arriving at this moment, uncertain what lay ahead, but certain of the effect it would have on me.

I watched as the Muslim passengers sitting near me laid down their rugs and prayed before boarding the plane. How wonderful it would be I thought, if we could all have a conversation about the world, about the differences in our faith, but how we could all love each other, all the children of God.

Destination: Holy Land

"United Airlines flight 140, nonstop, Chicago to Tel Aviv, now boarding……."

I looked around. For many passengers, this would be a return home. For others, perhaps a return visit. For me and my group, the trip of a lifetime. And before I knew it, we were roaring down the runway at nearly 200 miles per hour, lifting into the air…….

My faith journey began as a small child, walking up the steps to the Ingalls Park Methodist Church in Joliet, Illinois. I began reading the Bible by my teenage years, and always became curious by questions I could not find answers to. The Old Testament stories sometimes became hard to remember, but the New Testament, with Jesus, became light to my eyes. I yearned for more, again for answers that were not in the back of the book.

And soon I learned in life that not everyone believed in what I believed in. In fact, some did not believe at all.

"You may unbuckle your seat belts……."

I was jolted back to reality in my aisle seat. Sitting next to me was a Muslim woman with her young son. I had nodded to her when I sat down. Do I say something? Fourteen hours is a long time.

"Hello, my name is Bob," I said quietly, smiling.

"Safiya," she said, and then quickly turned to the window. I did not want to make her uncomfortable. I closed my eyes, knowing sleep was out of the question.

I knew I would see things that I had dreamed of, places I had seen portrayed in movies, and I knew there would be more, things that I knew nothing about. I wanted to see everything, but I also wanted to meet people, people just like me who were making their bucket list trip, and people completely unlike me, people who saw the world through different eyes. Could I have any of those conversations?

I looked at Safiya, and knew it would be difficult.

"What is the one thing you want to see most?" one of my sons had asked me before leaving.

I had actually given this much thought. You start with the manger scene, would there really be a cave? I envisioned a Holiday Inn likely sitting now in Bethlehem. Could I walk his walk along the Jordan River, was there a spot where he met John the Baptist, and could I be baptized there? Where did he find Peter and John and make them fishers of men? Could I kneel in that cove of the Galilee? I imagined being in the last supper room. And then of course the walk to Calvary, seeing a cross, and then a tomb.

I gave all these answers to my son.

"Yeah, I know dad," he said. "But which one?"

And I knew the answer. It was none of the above.

"Gethsemane," I told him. "It has been in my mind forever."

As that teenager reading the Bible, I remember Jesus praying in that garden, asking for the cup to be taken from him. He was afraid. Through all his greatness, this was Jesus as a human, just like I am, with human feelings. From every night since those teenage years, when I pray, I picture myself praying in that garden. I am with him. I too am asking God for help.

I closed my eyes, saw myself in Gethsemane, and smiled. And then sleep came.

"Good morning, breakfast?" The stewardess was asking.

I went with the scrambled eggs with chives. Safiya chose the quiche.

"Good Morning Safiya," I said quietly.

"Good morning, Bob," she answered.

I watched her wake up her son, and learned his name was Amir. He was around seven or eight years old, and I watched as they played tic-tac-toe on some paper. Of course, Safiya made sure Amir was winning. After a few minutes, I pulled out my own notebook, drew up a tic-tac-toe diagram, placed an X in a box, and handed it to Amir. He looked at his mother and me. She nodded and he placed an O. I placed another strategic X. Another O from Amir, excitedly. I somehow poorly placed another X. And then Amir had me.

"Tic Tac Toe!" he hollered triumphantly.

I had him give me a high five.

Safiya smiled. "Thank you, Bob."

I nodded. A nice, small victory to start the day.

We walked off the plane together when Safiya turned back to look at me.

"Enjoy your day, Bob" she said.

Of course this day was eight hours ahead of the old day, so it was already in the middle of the afternoon when we arrived in Tel Aviv. I quickly gathered with my small group, and we made our way through the Ben Gurion Airport. I glanced at every food and drink stand as we passed by.

"Forget it, Bob," Gene Couri said. "No Mountain Dew in Israel."

That would be Doctor Gene Couri, advising me of what lay ahead.

"Probably a good thing," he said.

"No it is not," I pouted.

Gretta, Marybeth, Aggie, Ilda, Lolly, Diana and Delores with a K all seemed to enjoy my predicament.

"Would you like some water, Bob?" Ilda asked with a big smile.

"Pass!" I said stubbornly.

We walked through a heavily secured airport, and then into a blistering hot August day. We all gathered into a van driven by Abu, and headed north, to Haifa, where our journey would begin before it ended in Jerusalem. There would be much to be seen in between. I was interested in the land, the history and the people.

I watched the landscape roll by. The never ending spectacle of white concrete buildings built into the hillside. It was certainly a different world.

"Bob," Abu hollered back to me. "I have water if you are thirsty."

And everyone laughed.

Abu headed west on Route 1 toward the Mediterranean, then north on Route 20. I had made notes of my journey before I left, and realized we were passing the Afeka Caves, an ancient Samaritan burial ground that was sitting in the middle of a residential area.

On my right came a return to the modern area, a huge shopping complex with flashing signs hollering Foot Locker, American Eagle and Nautica.

"This is Herzliya," Abu told us.

We passed a city called Yakum, where I saw a sign pointing to "Nude Beach." That would definitely not be part of my itinerary.

We were now on Route 2. A large city was in front of us, which I knew would be Netanya. The drive was beautiful now, heading north, the Mediterranean Sea to our left.

And then, Caesarea, the first place I really wanted to see in the Holy Land. This is where Jesus met with his disciples, where Peter declared him "The Christ, the Son of the Living God." It is where Jesus promised Peter, "the keys of the kingdom of heaven."

And it was where Paul was imprisoned for two years, writing his letters, with Luke at his side.

And then we were in Haifa, a booming city tucked right on the shore of the Mediterranean, nestled next to the ancient slopes of Mount Carmel.

"People do try to get along here, right?" I asked Abu as I left the van.

He smiled.

"I think they try."

I came to find out. Christians, Jews, and Muslims all in one spot.

"Bob," Abu said, holding me a bottle. "Don't forget your water."
Let the journey begin.

"Live for the moments you can't put into words."

CHAPTER 2

Haifa

"In Haifa, by the sea, the smells of salt rise from the earth. And the sun hanging from a tree unravels wind."

"Searching for Mountain Dew in Wadi Nisnas"

Ironically, I began my trip looking for a place of peace after hundreds of years of hatred.

Haifa

"Your only hope is in Haifa," I was told.

There is an old saying in Israel: "Haifa works, Jerusalem prays and Tel Aviv plays."

If you are looking for sacred places, you are in the wrong spot. It is one reason why people of different faiths can live together.

But I was following the footsteps, in real time, of Jesus. Our Lord was never in Haifa, a northern city sitting on the banks of the Mediterranean near the Carmel Mountains. But when our group decided to leave a few days early, we headed to Haifa.

It is a Jewish community, sprinkled with Christians and Muslims. And smack in the middle of it is a tiny, off the beaten path neighborhood called Wadi Nisnas. You won't find many tourists here, and in fact, without a guide, you would have trouble finding the neighborhood through the small winding roads and alleys.

A man walking next to me watched as I looked around.

"They call this the Mongoose Valley," he said.

It is sprinkled with outside markets and tiny restaurants. It feels like an older Arab neighborhood, with traditional ethnic stores. There is laffa flatbread, fresh salmon, halva, fresh vegetables and ground coffee.

Men stand behind the counters. Women sit on chairs hollering out the day's special items.

"Zucchini!" I hear.

I looked around as people from different cultures appeared to be mingling. Perhaps guarded, but friendly. It appears there are mostly Arab homes in the old stone houses of the neighborhood. Haifa might be mainly Jewish, but Wadi Nisnas felt Muslim with a spattering of Christians, densely populated and certainly lower income than the large, modern city surrounding it.

I slowly stepped up to one of the stores, a visitor out of place. Waiting customers were being given a treat.

"It's a falafel ball," a woman told me. "They dip them in tahini. Here, please try."

I tried a small ball. It is crunchy and light.

But I was not here for the falafel ball. I wanted to know how people of such different faiths and cultures could co-exist here, when they could not co-exist elsewhere.

Jesus was never here. Moses was never here. Mohammad was never here.

But their followers are.

I met Talia Goldberg, a student at the University of Haifa, outside the Wadi Nisnas Market along Yohanan Hakadosh Street. The smell of Coffee Mustafa drew us across the street. Talia told me she was a tour guide for a Jewish agency.

"People here are trying really hard," she said. "Especially the younger people. It is not perfect. There is so much work to be done. But it is better here than in other cities."

The neighborhood is a collection of Muslims and Christians, but some Jews live here too. I walked past Smile-N-Donuts, which was screaming my name, but I wanted the local flavor, so I kept walking. I saw my collection of the Couri family ahead of me and then looked at the street sign in front of me.

Khuri Street.

What are the chances?

I poked my head into Falafel George where a young boy was passing out free olives. Nobody was speaking English, but everyone was smiling. I made my way back down Hakadosh Street to Elias Vegetable Shop. In front of the store a woman sitting on a bench greeted me warmly. I told her I was writing a book about my trip.

"Welcome to our store," she said. "I am Umm Elias. What do you like to eat?"

I smiled and pointed to my belly. She laughed. I asked her about her name. She said Umm means mother in Arabic, and Abu means father. She walked me into the store.

"I have something you will like," she said. "Here, have you tried this?"

I looked at what Umm brought before me.

"What is it?" I asked.

"Bull's tongue!" she smiled.

I looked in horror.

"Give me an orange," I told her. "I am in the mood for a good orange."

"But you said you wanted to experience Haifa?" she laughed.

"I do," I said. "Maybe I will later."

I think Umm knew that was a lie.

I caught back up with my group, orange in hand. I needed to find the Beit-Hagefen Arab Jewish Center.

It was built in 1963 with one goal: bringing Arabs and Jews together, and helping them coexist. It meant education. It meant tolerance. It meant acceptance. There are cultural and artistic activities. There are festivals. There are community meetings.

What could not happen elsewhere is happening in Haifa. And Wadi Nisnas is at the heart of it.

Asaf Ron is the Executive Director at Beit-Hagefen. He is Jewish.

"My friends are always surprised about our city," Asaf told me. "I tell them it is easier to bring people together with culture than debates."

I told Asaf I had just walked the streets of Wadi Nisnas.

"This is a place where people can express their opinions. If there is anger, they can express it. But it does not lead to violence."

"What happens when it does?" I asked him.

"We want people to get to know each other," he said. "If a problem occurs, let's talk about it. You do not have to agree. You do not have to understand. But you do have to listen. People must understand each other and care for each other."

Asaf paused and looked out his window toward the city.

"Our biggest challenge is building trust and reducing fear. We are trying to lower the level of the water. And that is what changes the world," he smiled.

I reminded him that he was dealing with centuries of handed down religious hatred, a subject not lost upon anyone in the streets of Haifa, or the markets in Wadi Nisnas.

"This is our history now," he said. "Haifa is making history. It is our DNA. Nothing can happen without education."

I asked Asaf if Christians and Jews and Arabs, after walking the streets and coexisting during the day, can ever break bread and be friends together at night.

That drew a chuckle.

"No," he smiled. "That rarely happens. They do not do things together. There is fear as to how that might look to others. There are language problems. People want to stay within their own communities, speak in their own languages, have their own holidays, learn about their own history and religion. And yet while they are not going out together, you hear both Arabic and English in the streets. Jews and Arabs know each other. They just don't meet each other. And then when there is a conflict......"

"What happens?" I ask.

Asaf smiled again.

"Let's just say things are better here than other places."

With that, we shook hands and I told Asaf I had great respect for his efforts, and appreciated his time.

He nodded.

"Tell them we honor everyone who lives here," he said, firmly shaking my hand. "People here want to live harmoniously. This is a special place, considering."

And then he paused.

"The Jews and Arabs could sign a peace agreement tomorrow, but the people would still not be ready to meet each other. Too many years. Too much hatred."

Abu Adam is an Arab from Nazareth. He drives American tourists through Israel. One of seven children, he has witnessed the good and the bad of the three cultures.

"I have been around Jews and Christians and Muslims my whole life. I grew up with them. I think for the most part, we get along well. But we keep to our own."

Ayob Farah has also seen it all. He was born in a Jewish populated Haifa, grew up in a Muslim populated Nazareth, and now lives in Wadi Nisnas, studying law at the University, and working as a tour guide.

"I am Christian," he says. "If you are Arabic, it is fine. We do not care. But sometimes your neighbor is your enemy. And usually, you are very similar. You can either be divided by the world or shape the world together."

I asked him to compare Haifa to other parts of Israel.

"People do not get in your face here," he said. "It is much easier in Haifa."

Sitting next to Ayob on the American tour bus is his grandfather Anton, widely considered a legend in Israel history. He is pushing 90 now, and has spent the past 50 years walking the hills of Nazareth, Bethlehem and Jerusalem teaching tourists about Holy Land history.

"They call him 'The Walking Encyclopedia,'" Ayob proudly says.

Anton was born in a Christian village in Galilee, and holds academic degrees in education, geography and literature. He is fluent in Arabic, Hebrew and English. He learned long ago that you have to go along to get along in the MIddle East.

"The Jewish problem today is the same problem it was two thousand years ago, and probably will be two thousand years from now. Nobody can talk to anybody."

I listened close as we shared a bottle of orange Fanta.

"To live here, you have to know how to balance between all three religions. Sometimes, you are next to somebody who loves you. Millions of times, you are not. And if you are not, you will not have an easy time. To feel safe here, you have to smile, and live your life on lies."

"As in pretending?" I ask.

"Yes," Anton answered. "Except in Haifa. In Haifa, nobody looks at the color of your eyes."

> *"There in Haifa, by the sea, at the end*
> *of the summer that broke on the treetop,*
> *a moon unfurled. I return to the*
> *silence I had split with my lips."*

CHAPTER 3

Elijah's Cave

"The Lord said to Elijah, "Go, stand in front of me on the mountain, and I will pass by you." Then a very strong wind blew until it caused the mountains to fall apart and large rocks to break in front of the Lord. But the Lord was not in the wind. After the wind, there was an earthquake, but the Lord was not in the earthquake. After the earthquake, there was a fire, but the Lord was not in the fire. After the fire, there was a quiet, gentle sound. When Elijah heard it, he covered his face with his coat and went out and stood at the entrance to the cave. Then a voice said to him, "Elijah! Why are you here?" He answered, " Lord God All-Powerful, I have always served you as well as I could. But the people of Israel have broken their agreement with you, destroyed your altars, and killed your prophets with swords. I am the only prophet left, and now they are trying to kill me, too.""

Our journey into the Holy Land begins in the 8th century, BC, with Elijah's stand against the prophets of Baal. The spot where Elijah challenged them is called Muhraka. It is at the peak of Mount Carmel in Haifa. From there you can see the Jezreel Valley.

We drove down Allenby Road, on Mount Carmel, to see the cave where Elijah lived, and is considered one of the most sacred caves in the Holy Land. Christians, Jews and Muslims all gather here to pray, as the cave has long been a place to seek miracles. Sick people arrive in hopes of being cured, and Mary, Joseph and baby Jesus hid here when they fled from Egypt.

There are actually two caves here for praying, one for men and one for women. And right above the caves is the Stella Maris Monastery along Tchernichovsky Street, a Christian Church built in the 19th century.

"Stella Maris" means "Star of the Sea," and was named for Mary.

You drive up the highway and see the cave literally hanging over the road. You wonder how the structure and landscape has changed over generations, 29 centuries since Elijah hid inside. The cave is about 45 yards up the slope of the mountain.

And on this day, the Jews and Christians were not getting along.

The Breslov Hasidic's, a Jewish group believes Elisha, the successor to Elijah, is buried inside the monastery, and they want to pray there. The Christians believe Elisha is buried in Samaria, about 70 miles away. And while Christians and Jews pray together at other holy sites, like the Western Wall and King David's tomb, Jewish prayer at what the Christians consider just their site did not go over well.

The monastery now had a locked gate, fencing around it, and a guard at the gate.

"This has been going on for a couple of months now," he told me. "We have had scuffles and even physical violence."

"How many serious instances?" I asked.

"Around ten," he said.

The monastery is considered one of the oldest monasteries in the world, dating back to 1291 AD. Mount Carmel is not really a single mountain, but more like a mountain ridge, reaching 1,700 feet above sea level. It is thickly wooded, and was a hiding point in ancient time for criminals. This is where David stayed before he became king.

The Bible says the cave was on the slope of the mountain. The cave is almost hidden under the tip of Mount Carmel. As you look up from ground level, there is only one noticeable cave, and it sits on the front of the mountain. There is a stone statue of Elijah, seen raising his sword to Baal's prophets, his foot stomping a man's head. Engraved in the main doorway is the inscription "With zeal have I been zealous for the Lord God of Hosts."

The striking white church is built in the shape of a cross, with a bell tower and a dome decorated with paintings from both the Old and New Testament. You see Elijah rising to the heavens, and David playing his harp. A statue of the Virgin Mary rests over the altar, and there are dozens of Greek inscriptions on the walls. The inside is both dark and small.

Destination: Holy Land

I walked around the monastery, pen and paper in hand, taking notes the old fashioned way. A nun spotted me and quietly approached me.

"Are you from the newspaper?" she asked.

"No," I said smiling. "I am an American tourist, writing about the Holy Land."

We spoke for a few moments. I asked her about the violence at the holy site.

"We had to put guards by the entrance," she says. "It is for our own safety."

"Very sad," I tell her.

"This has been a sacred place for Christians for centuries," she said.

As we talked, a man who was standing by the gate approached us, obviously concerned about the nun.

"It is okay," she told him. "His name is Bob."

We shook hands. I asked him about watching the gate, and whether things really were better in Haifa.

"This is not how we act in Haifa," he said. "We live here side by side without problems. And then they come and start this."

Ironically, it is mostly an Arab-Jewish skirmish outside the Christian site. Such is life in the battle of cultures waged over thousands of years. But today, it was peaceful. If the demonstrators were there, it was not apparent. Worshipers coming out of Stella Maris showed no signs of knowing what had been happening recently.

I stood next to a Jewish man and watched people coming and going.

"At least it is peaceful today," he said. We made small talk. He told me his name was Elijah, and smiled at my reaction.

"Yes," he said. "The cave has special meaning to me and my family."

"Do you usually get along with the Arabs?" I asked him.

"There are usually no problems here," he said. "This is stupid. We both worship the cave. We pray. They pray. Stupid."

We shook hands and said goodbye. "The cave is important to Christians too," he said. "I hope you enjoyed your visit."

I assured him I did, and that I would not soon forget meeting Elijah at Elijah's Cave.

We were just minutes from the Mediterranean, where the rest of my group had ventured to take pictures. I wandered next door to the Kalamaris Restaurant, looking to make one more friend before leaving Haifa. A woman named Michelle greeted me at the entrance.

"One for lunch?" she asked.

"No," I smiled. "I am an American visiting, writing a book about Haifa, and about how people get along here."

She laughed. "You picked a bad time. But it seems to have quieted down. I hope we can get back to normal."

I looked through the restaurant at the beautiful views outside.

"We have fresh sea bass today," Michelle said.

I smiled and shook my head no.

"Everyone is welcome here?" I asked.

"Yes," she said. "Everyone is welcome everywhere in Haifa."

Just not recently across the street.

I kept walking to the Santa Maria Restaurant. The sign outside claimed Austrian food. I could tell language was going to be a problem here, but it did not matter. My nose was working just fine, and I was staring at a warm piece of apple strudel that I soon found to be wonderful. I was sure on that topic that Christians, Muslims and Jews could all agree.

I caught back up with our tour group. I listened as both Anton and Ayob told us about the area, and my local group talk about the beauty they had seen at the Mediterranean. They asked what I had been up to. I rubbed my stomach and said, "apple strudel, from Austria."

As we prepared to leave Haifa, I looked one last time: a beautiful modern city overlooking the Mediterranean Sea; Jews, Muslims and Christians walking safely in the streets; the smell of shawarma's and bureka's in the air. It was perfect. I had visited with Christians, Muslims, and Jews, and could not have been welcomed more warmly,

On this day at least, Haifa still shined as the beacon light on top of the mountain.

The bus pulled out and I thought back to Elijah. He believed all the prophets had failed, and he was the last believer left on earth. He was in a low, dark place. And there came God.

Right where I was in Haifa.

> *"God answered with a spectacular display of fire from heaven, consuming the offering, licking up the sodden wood as well as every drop of water that had been poured over the altar. Even the rocks of the altar were consumed. The people fell on their faces, proclaiming, "The Lord, he is God; the Lord, he is God."*

CHAPTER 4

The Wailing Wall

"In the four hundred and eightieth year after the Israelites came out of Egypt, in the fourth year of Solomon's reign over Israel, in the month of Ziv, the second month, he began to build the temple of the Lord. The temple that King Solomon built for the Lord was sixty cubits long, twenty wide and thirty high."

"Praying at the Wailing Wall"

The Wailing Wall

I very much looked forward to visiting the Western, or Wailing Wall. If ever there was a place where people of different religions and cultures could gather together in prayer, this was it. The Wall is the most visited site in Israel. It only closes on Jewish holidays. It is the last remaining outer wall of the ancient Jewish temple. It is considered the holiest site where Jews are allowed to pray. Some 15 million people visit the Wall every year. And while most are Orthodox Jews, tourists and pilgrims flock there daily.

It is called the Wailing Wall for the Jewish cries out to God, praying for the arrival of the Savior. The Wall got its name from small water drops. Legend has it the Wall would get covered with small drops of water that resembled tear drops. There has never been a scientific explanation for the arrival of the drops.

And Muslims believe this is the site where Mohammed rose to heaven when he left the earth.

For everyone here, it is a connection to God. After all, this is where the creation of the world happened. It was Mount Moriah then, and is the Temple Mount now. This is where Abraham offered Isaac as a sacrifice to the Lord. That is how you measure your faith in God.

The original Temple was built under King Solomon. King Herod would flatten Mount Moriah and build the second Temple walls in 20 BC, but the Romans destroyed it, along with the rest of Jerusalem, in 70 AD. But Herod's huge stones remained as the foundation, forming seven layers of bricks, and as centuries passed, the location of the Wall is where Jews would gather to pray. The wall is made with Jerusalem limestone, and rises over 100 feet high, with much of it located below street level in tunnels. The oldest, gigantic, Herod era bricks for the bottom. The further the wall goes up, the smaller the bricks become in the passage of centuries.

While the temple has been rebuilt many times, you look at those giant bricks on the bottom, and you understand. The Wall is the only remaining part of that second Temple, and sits roughly 100 yards from where the original Temple stood.

Today, you walk into the sacred ground and the first thing you notice are the Israeli soldiers. Young, many of them women, carrying rifles. And then you see them. People in deep prayer everywhere, standing and touching the walls, or on their knees rocking back and forth. You watch as they write messages and prayers on little pieces of paper, and stuff them in the crevices of the rocks. You notice that men and women are separated.

I again ask someone, why?

Destination: Holy Land

"The men have to pray," I am told. "The women do not."

Seemed odd, I thought. But that was nothing compared to what had happened recently at the Wall.

Hundreds of far-right Meuhadim Jews staged a protest at the Wall over what they described as Christian worship at the holy site. The protests got so out of hand police had to shove the protesters out of the way just so visitors could walk through the doors.

"Missionaries Go Home!" they shouted.

Leading the group was Jerusalem Deputy Mayor Aryeh King, who told those gathered, "As far as I am concerned, let every missionary know they are not welcome in the Land of Israel."

With that, the protesters began hurling insults and spitting on visitors.

And the battle of the religions did not stop there.

The Israeli government put forward a bill that would ban mixed prayer anywhere at the Western Wall. The proposal would have criminalized the activity of the Women of the Wall prayer group, and banned visitors from wearing certain clothing. Playing music or singing songs would be a criminal offense. They proposed jail time and steep fines. The goal was to shut down any mixed prayer areas. Guards began searching visitors for Torah scrolls and books.

Fortunately, that all stopped.

But no matter how frustrating times can be, we stop and realize why we are here, and remember that our Lord and Savior Jesus Christ stood here before us.

When our Lord was just 40 days old, Mary and Joseph brought him to the temple to fulfill the command in the Torah. Luke tells us Jesus went there every year as he grew up. When he was 12, Mary and Joseph took him to the temple to celebrate Passover. He was accidently left behind, and spent his time asking questions of the rabbi's there. Later in life he taught there frequently, and of course when he entered just days before his death, he overturned the sellers' tables.

On this day, there was an impressive section of different Jewish sects praying at the wall. You see them weeping, crying, shouting prayers and reciting Torah. You watch them pray and you realize that they put faith before politics.

Then you watch them get up to leave, walking backwards, never taking their eyes off the Wall.

I ask a person standing next to me why?

The Wailing Wall

"Because it is disrespectful to turn away," I am told.

Their devotion hits your heart and gut. You feel humbled. You wonder if your faith is as strong as theirs.

I watched as Orthodox Jews, Conservative Jews, Reform Jews and Hassidic Jews came and went.

Ayob approached me as I was taking notes.

"Do you know about the tunnels?" he asked me.

"Tunnels?" I asked.

Ayob waved his grandfather over.

Tunnels?" I asked again.

The encyclopedia smiled.

"They go under the Muslim quarter," Anton said. "They date to the Second Temple, which was destroyed about 2,000 years ago. You can see about 75 yards of it."

The grandfather and grandson looked at me.

"I think you came here to do something," Ayob said.

I nodded, and began my journey toward the wall. People were everywhere. I looked for an open spot where I could pray in private. I did not want to stand out, did not want to offend any of the regulars or their customs. This was a profound Jewish site. I was a mere visitor, and wanted to be respectful. I felt a man tug my arm.

"Come," he said. "Here is a good spot."

His name was Daniel, and he told me he came to the wall to pray three times a day. He asked about my prayer routine.

"Nothing like yours," I said. "I feel like I talk to God throughout the day, usually in quiet moments. But this……"

"Listen," he said. "What do you hear?"

I heard everything. People mumbling quietly, others chanting loudly.

"Exactly," he said. "Us Jews are all different. We pray to the same God, but we do it differently."

I asked him how he felt about Christians and Muslims praying at the wall.

"Well" he said, "early Christians would have prayed here. We see Muslim visitors here, but not as much praying."

I listened to the chants.

"Tehillms," Daniel said.

He could tell I did not know what that meant.

"Like Christian Psalms, or poems. We have about 150 of them. Those are the chants you hear."

I kept listening.

"O God, the heathen are come into thine inheritance; thy holy temple have they defiled; they have laid Jerusalem on heaps.......So we thy people and sheep of thy pasture will give thee thanks for ever: we will shew forth thy praise to all generations."

Daniel saw I was ready.

"Thank you," I said, holding out my hand.

"Shalom," he said, smiling.

"Shalom," I answered.

And then I took a few steps forward, touched the wall, and dropped to my knees. I did not have any Psalms memorized, or any prayer pre-planned. For a moment, I just sat in silence, thinking about how many people knelt in this spot before me. And then it became natural, just a private, quiet moment between me and God. I thanked him for dropping Daniel onto my lap.

Then I gathered myself, stood up, and walked back to my group. I nodded at the young women holding rifles. I saw Ayob and Anton smiling at me. My group of Couri's were huddled together.

"Bob," Marybeth said, "how did it feel to kneel at the wall and pray?"

"I need to learn the Tehillim's," I smiled.

As we left, I looked back into the crowd for Daniel. He was talking to another man, likely having the same conversation he had earlier with me. A Jew teaching a Christian how to pray at their holy site.

A gift from God.

"The word of the Lord came to Solomon: "As for this temple you are building, if you follow my decrees, observe my laws and keep all my commands

and obey them, I will fulfill through you the promise I gave to David your father. And I will live among the Israelites and will not abandon my people Israel."

CHAPTER 5

Beit Sahour

"Don't urge me to leave you or to turn back from you. Where you go I will go, and where you stay I will stay. Your people will be my people and your God my God. Where you die I will die, and there I will be buried. May the Lord deal with me, be it ever so severely, if even death separates you and me."

And we meet Ruth in the Old Testament, as she is talking to her mother-in-law Naomi, teaching us how the Lord intervened to protect the family line of David so he would eventually become King. In the fields of Beit Sahour Ruth would go into the fields to find grain, gleaning kernels from the barley harvest. She would eventually meet Boaz, and all became right in the world again.

Beit Sahour is now a Palestinian town, just east of Bethlehem, one of the few cities in the Holy Land still dominated by Christians. The town dates back to 3000 BC. But the times have long been changing, and Beit Sahour has become a center of political activism, and is now under the administration of the Palestinian National Authority.

I looked out the window as our bus rolled down Al Quds Street. I had studied the geography, and I knew the Shepherd's Field was minutes away, and Bethlehem was just down the street. It was real now.

Our tour bus pulled into the Beit Sahour Souvenir Store, the best souvenir shop we found in the Holy Land, featuring handcrafted olive wood made in Bethlehem. Aisle after aisle of jewelry and perfume awaited your credit card. And behind the counter was the master ring leader, Joseph Kassis, who runs the store with his adult children.

"I am writing a book about my trip to the Holy Land," I told him as he hustled his way between customers. "Could I ask you a few questions?"

Kassis agreed, and we sat down for a few minutes to talk.

"This store is my family business," he told me. "It is our life."

Joseph opened his store in 2010 with his sons George and Fadi. When covid struck, business stopped. But they were back open now, and Kassis was beaming. I asked him about Christian's in the area.

"We are here to preserve the Christian minority in the Holy Land," he said, pounding the table with a passion.

As we chatted about life in Beit Sahour, I told Kassis I was curious why there were so few Christians in the Holy Land, and why the few that remained had settled in Beit Sahour. I wanted to know what made his city different? 100 years ago, everyone in Beit Sahour was Christian. Today, that number is down to 80%, with an influx of Muslim residents making up the other 20%. Still, the small town is a beacon of light in dwindling Christian darkness.

He smiled. "Christians that still live here are our heroes," Kassis said. "But yes, the numbers, they are rapidly dwindling. You see what has happened over time. The Muslims have moved into our land. It will not stop. I do not know how many Christians will be left here 30 years from now. There are just too many problems for a Christian family living in the Holy Land today. Why would they stay if they do not have to?"

Kassis could see that I did not understand.

"Look," he says. "I am friends with everyone here. Christians and Muslims. But If I have to go to the government for something, I have to deal with Muslims in the Palestinian Authority. And they make me feel like I am a second class citizen. It is terrible."

I told Kassis how impressive his family run store was.

"Our store is very important to Beit Sahour," he says. "Everyone knows we are here. It preserves our Christian spirit and history in difficult times."

There are really only two Christian dominated towns still remaining in the Holy Land, Beit Sahour and Taybeh, 60 miles to the north. But incidents in Taybeh have caused concern. In 2005, Muslim men from nearby Deir Jarir torched homes in Taybeh after word of an affair spread between Muslim woman from Deir Jarir and a Christian man from Taybeh.

"We get along better than most," Kassis said.

Beit Sahour

I thanked him for his time, and headed outside for one of the highlights of my trip, where I was meeting Bassam and Hiyam Bannoura, who lived in Beit Sahour. Their daughter Sada is one of my dear friends back home. I spent hours listening to her stories about growing up in Bethlehem. When I told her I was going to the Holy Land, she had heard enough.

"I am face timing them right now," she said.

And with that, I knew that we had to meet.

We greeted, exchanged gifts, told stories about Sada, and laughed the time away.

I told them about my conversation with Joseph Kassis. They both nodded in agreement.

"Our Christian population is shrinking," Bassam said.

"Why?" I asked. "This is where the shepherd's announced the birth of Jesus. This really is the Holy Land."

"There are two major problems for Christians living here," Bassam said. "First is the policies of the Israeli government."

"And second," I wondered.

"Muslim fundamentalism," Bassam said.

"I am not sure how you fix either of those in today's world," I said.

Bassam still lives in the Beit Sahour area where his ancestors were the town's very first missionaries. But as a teenager, he was an atheist. Then by his mid-20's, he accepted Jesus Christ as his Lord and Savior.

I told him that must have been a remarkable journey.

"Yes," he said. "I read the Muslim book of the Quran. But I eventually realized that their God was not a God that I could follow. He was angry, evil and vengeful. So I enrolled at Bethlehem Bible College, not really knowing what I believed in."

"Did they know you were an atheist?" I asked.

Bassam smiled. "I hid it from everyone."

"So what happened?" I asked.

"The Lord was talking to me, pushing me, guiding me. And then one night I opened my Bible and it fell to John 12:8."

"The poor," I said.

"Yes," said Bassam, "the poor. Jesus told the disciples 'The poor you have with you always. Me you do not have always.'"

We paused and looked at each other.

"That pierced my heart," he said. "Jesus knew 2,000 years ago that the poor will always be with us."

"He did," I said.

We grasped hands.

"I wasted years of my life as an atheist," he said. "Forty years ago I was brought to my knees. And I have never turned back from Jesus."

Bassam and Hiyam took their family to Indiana, where he studied in the Seminary. He returned to his West Bank city and taught Greek at the Bible School. Today, Bassam is the Pastor of the Shepherd's Field Evangelical Church in Beit Sahour.

"For Christians, faith begins right here," Bassam said. "In the Shepherd's Field, and in that manger in Bethlehem. Faith is the key to our lives."

Praise God.

We hugged and said goodbye. I now had two friends, halfway around the world. What a fantastic hour of my life this was.

Praise God again.

We still had time to kill, so I joined some others walking down the street to the Citadel Cafe. We sat on a patio outside and I looked at the wall above me.

"If we fail to defend our just cause, then we should change the defenders, not the cause."

A waiter named Mahmoud came to wait on us. I asked him what it was like to live in Beit Sahour under Palestinian rule.

"We do not have independence," he said. "We do not have land. We do not have freedom. They will not let us travel. There are no jobs. How can we get better?"

I asked him if he ever thought about leaving.

"No," he said. "This is my home."

"But many others have left," I said.

"Yes, they have left," he said, shaking his head. "But I will stay."

It was a reminder that even on this great day, there was a feeling of uncertainty in the air of Palestinian rule. In the area around the birthplace of Jesus, there are about a quarter of a million people. Only about 30,000 of them are Christians.

We got up to leave and I went to shake Mahmoud's hand.

"Our heritage," he said. "Our land."

And with that, we left Beit Sahour. It was time to begin tracing the steps of Jesus. We would soon return to the Shepherd's Field, and then, Bethlehem and a manger scene.

But first back to Nazareth.

Beit Sahour

"But you Bethlehem Ephrathah, who are too little to be among the clans of Judah, from you shall come forth for me one who is to be ruler of Israel."

CHAPTER 6

The Church of Annunciation

"In the sixth month the angel Gabriel was sent by God to a town in Galilee called Nazareth, to a virgin engaged to a man whose name was Joseph, of the house of David. The virgin's name was Mary. And he came to her and said, "Hail, full of grace! The Lord is with you." But she was much perplexed by his words and pondered what sort of greeting this might be. The angel said to her, "Do not be afraid, Mary, for you have found favor with God. And now, you will conceive in your womb and bear a son, and you will name him Jesus. He will be great, and will be called the Son of the Most High, and the Lord God will give to him the throne of his ancestor David. He will reign over the house of Jacob forever, and of his kingdom there will be no end."

"Where it all begins"

The Church of Annunciation

Our first stop in Nazareth was the most important one: The Church of Annunciation, where it all began, when the angel Gabriel visited Mary. The church is the largest church in the Middle East, towering over the city. The current church was built in 1967, the fifth time the church was built over the site. They say the stairs from the original church date back to the 4th century.

There were probably about 50 carved houses made of stone when Jesus grew up in Nazareth. Those homes would have been right where The Church of Annunciation stands today. I was now standing where he surely did.

Approaching the church, you are struck by its size and modern shape. It is two stories tall. The upper level is the church, the lower level is Mary's grotto. Outside the church are gates with scenes from the Old Testament. There is Adam and Eve; next to them are Noah and the arc; then Abraham and the sacrifice of Isaac. I followed the gates around the church to another entrance, where I found New Testament scenes, from Jesus being baptized to the crucifixion.

With my earlier stops behind me, I was already wondering if I was really prepared for the emotions that I knew were coming. I sat for a moment and reflected. I knew I had longed for this, and I would likely never pass this way again. I said a quick prayer, then entered on the southern side of the church. There stood a statue of Mary when she was young, around 14. Her hands are now black from all of the tourists who have touched her. A bronze statue of Jesus awaits you upon entering.

Other people were hurriedly passing by me. I just stood and stared at Jesus.

"Hello again, Bob."

I was jolted back to reality, and saw a man I met earlier named Steve from our group. He was also writing about his trip. He was smiling.

"Are you ready for this?" he asked me.

I smiled. "I'm ready." I said. "Let's go."

And we walked inside. And I said to myself, "Bob, keep it together."

The church was dimly lit. The first thing I noticed were all the drawings of Mary in different forms. There was a Spanish Mary, a black Mary, and an Asian Mary. I looked down and saw the floors, made of marble. They had names of all the Pope's engraved in them.

As much as I appreciated the church, what I came to see was on the bottom floor, the grotto, the place that Pilgrims called "Mary's house," and the spot where Gabriel arrived.

And of course, this was the site of the turning point of humanity.

Above the door of the cave is inscribed the Latin phrase "Verbum caro factum est et habitavit in nobis."

It means "The Word was made flesh and dwelt among us."

I was writing down the inscription when someone tugged my arm, and pointed me at another one.

"Chaire Maria."

What did it mean?

I listened as 'The Walking Encyclopedia,' Anton Ayob explained it to our group.

"During construction of the church," he began, "they found this small inscription. It means 'Hail Mary.'"

Anton paused.

"Chaire Maria, or Hail Mary," he said, "is exactly what Gabriel said to Mary."

And we have another moment where chills went down my spine.

I waited in line for my moment to approach the altar, the same spot where Gabriel approached Mary more than 2,000 years ago. In front of us was a group from Costa Rica, proudly wearing matching shirts. I looked behind us. A group from the Far East. And then it was our turn, and then mine.

There was no need for pen and paper now. This moment was between me and my Lord. As I knelt there, I soaked it all in, and I realized there would be many more.

Eyes closed, I pictured what I had lived in my mind hundreds of times. Gabriel, the voice, and a stunned Mary. How would any of us have reacted? I said a short prayer, gave thanks for this moment, and smiled.

I got up, climbed those old stairs, and made my way out of the church. I passed a nun as I left.

"Did you enjoy Mary's grotto?" she asked me.

"Yes ma'am, I sure did," I said.

"Did you know," she smiled, "that parents have named more daughters Mary than any other woman who has ever lived?"

"I know," I told her. "I know."

"And do you know why God chose Mary?" she asked, still smiling.

The Church of Annunciation

I paused and thought for a minute.

"God does not make mistakes," I said. "He could have chosen anyone. And he chose Mary for the most important job in the history of the world. She would bring us the Messiah."

"Just as Isaiah told us long ago," she said as she pulled out her bible and read to me.

"Therefore the Lord himself will give you a sign: The virgin will conceive and give birth to a son, and will call him Immanuel."

"Mary gave herself to God's mission," she said. "The virgin birth is God's power to do the impossible. Believing in God means believing that anything is possible. We call it faith, and it defines us."

I could have sat and listened to her words all day.

"It was nice to meet you," she said. "I must go back inside for mass."

I thanked her and prayed her wisdom would someday be mine.

With mass going on inside, I walked down Al-Bishara Street to the Sisters of the Nazareth Convent. Maybe there was more wisdom to be found. Inside I discovered a room full of clothing worn by Popes and Cardinals dating hundreds of years. The convent was actually a bed and breakfast now, sporting a modest guest house.

Back outside, I ventured down the street where a large crowd gathered at the Market Nazareth. It didn't take long before my eyes settled on Dewan al-Saraya, which I first thought was a restaurant, then realized it was also a museum of sorts. The owner was holding fort in the front, speaking to a group of visitors. They were talking about old coffee pots and clocks. I looked around and saw antiques everywhere. I watched as he kept speaking, non stop, while he was also serving customers.

"Abu, Abu!" people kept shouting his name. I learned his name was Abu Ashraf. I finally got his attention.

"Lemonade, with the mint," I said.

"No food?" he asked.

"No thanks," I said.

"You will try my katayef," he said.

I grimaced, and others began ribbing me.

"You must try Abu's katayef!"

Abu looked at me smiling. He knew he had me.

And the katayef was incredible. Basically a fried pancake stuffed with goodies and dunked in syrup.

Abu was watching closely. And then……

"I told you that you would like Abu's katayef!" he hollered for all to hear.

With my belly full, I headed back toward the church and waited for the crowd to finish mass. I saw my group come out.

"Steve," I said. "How was the mass?"

"Amazing," he said. "Did you keep yourself busy?"

"Nuns and katayef," I smiled.

We walked over and stood by the Mary statue. Other groups were pouring in.

"Amazing day," he said quietly.

"Amazing," I nodded.

And I know that over time, as I age, there will be things I might forget about my journey.

Being in the spot where Gabriel visited Mary will never be one of them.

"Mary said to the angel, "How can this be, since I am a virgin?" The angel said to her, "The Holy Spirit will come upon you, and the power of the Most High will overshadow you; therefore the child to be born will be holy; he will be called Son of God. And now, your relative Elizabeth in her old age has also conceived a son; and this is the sixth month for her who was said to be barren. For nothing will be impossible with God." Then Mary said, "Here am I, the servant of the Lord; let it be with me according to your word." Then the angel departed from her."

CHAPTER 7

Ein Karem-Church of the Visitation

"At that time Mary got ready and hurried to a town in the hill country of Judea, where she entered Zechariah's home and greeted Elizabeth. When Elizabeth heard Mary's greeting, the baby leaped in her womb, and Elizabeth was filled with the Holy Spirit."

"Mary's Well"

That town in the hill country of Judea where Mary visited is believed to be Ein Karem, a small Bohemian village of about 2,000 people that still oozes of old world charm. It is an ancient town, settled thousands of years before Mary arrived. Excavations there date to 2000 BC, with Jewish residents there in the first century.

Ein Karem means "Spring of the Vineyard." It is a little more than 5 miles west of Jerusalem, and as I look back on my journey, it may have been the most picturesque town I visited, seemingly untouched by modern conveniences, surrounded by vineyards, almond trees and gardens. It was a postcard magnet, with many old houses still preserved and lived in.

As our bus drove through the small town, and I sat in the comfort of a cushioned seat, relaxing in the air conditioning on a warm September day, I thought about Mary's journey to visit her much older cousin.

Her route from Nazareth to Ein Karem would span about 100 miles. Her donkey would have been moving about three miles per hour. So the trip took more than 30 hours. But it wasn't just the distance that Mary, stunned by her visit from Gabriel, and now carrying the baby Jesus, had to travel. Nazareth was just over 1,000 feet above sea level. But Ein Karem was more than doubled that, at about nearly 2,500 feet.

Mary didn't just go 100 miles. She went there uphill! And Elizabeth lived at the top of a mountain when she got there!

Pilgrims began coming in the 6th century as word spread about a spring where Mary is believed to have stopped for a drink of water. They dubbed it "Mary's Well."

As our bus arrived at the Church of the Visitation, believed to be the site of Zechariah and Elizabeth's summer house, one of the tourists saw me writing and said "Did you bring your walking shoes with you?"

Walking shoes? I winced. He obviously knew something that I did not. And that was not a good sign.

The bus parked, I got out, and I was immediately staring at a mountain. On top of it was a church.

It can't be, I thought.

"There probably isn't a chair lift going up there, is there?" I joked to a couple of tourists.

They laughed. "Don't think so."

We started climbing stairs, and I began counting. 25. 50. 75. 100.

People were passing me by.

125. 150. 175. And then......

Ein Karem - Church of the Visitation

I arrived, sadly one of the last from our group. I again prayed to God, this time giving him thanks for getting me there.

In the courtyard outside the church the streets are ancient. Nearby are alleys covered with murals. There are statues of Mary and Elizabeth greeting each other. If you look closely, it appears their bellies are touching. There is also a mural of Mary, riding a donkey, to commemorate her journey.

There is a wall opposite the church that contains plaques from Mary's song of praise, The Magnificat, that appears in Luke's Gospel. Incredibly, it is translated into 58 languages from around the world..

"Can you speak any of those," a woman next to me asked, as she watched me go from language to language.

"One," I said, pointing to the English version.

The church was built in the middle of the 20th century on the top of the ruins of many earlier churches destroyed over time. A sign welcoming visitors says "Custodia Terrae Sanctae," meaning "Custodians of the Holy Land," referencing the Franciscans who have stood watch over the church for 700 years.

The building itself is built similar to the Church of the Annunciation, with two levels, a church on top, and the crypt below. Inside the church are numerous beautiful murals of women from the Old Testament, and the church's columns also display the verses from Mary's Magnificat.

But like the Church of the Annunciation, what I wanted to see was downstairs, in the crypt, the spot where Mary met Elizabeth.

We entered the crypt and saw a passageway to a water well. I looked on confused as I was scribbling my notes.

"Mary's Well," a woman next to me whispered.

Anton, "The Walking Encyclopedia," heard her, looked at me, and then addressed the group.

"When Mary greeted Elizabeth," he said, "a spring burst out from these rocks. Mary and Elizabeth would have sat here, relaxed, talked, and drank from it."

And then Anton guided us over to a huge stone.

"This is the 'Stone of Hiding," he said. "During Herod's Massacre of the Innocents, this is where Zecharia and Elizabeth hid baby John. The stone opened, and they hid him inside."

Next to the stone is a painting on the wall of baby John hiding.

"Now come closer," Anton told the group. We all gathered in tightly.

"Look closely," Anton said. "What do you see?"

I saw an imprint in the wall, impossible to make out what it was, but it was something, maybe a foot long.

"It is the imprint of a young person's body," Anton said. "A baby."

Everyone looked at each other. Stunned silence. Another moment that takes your breath away.

We left the church and made our way back to the bus. I was writing notes furiously. The statues. The Magnificat. The well. The imprint. It was all here.

The walk back to the bus, downhill, was much easier.

"You doing okay Bob?" Ayob, Anton's grandson asked me.

"More than okay," I said. "This was another great moment of my life."

"Get ready for more," he said. "We are just beginning."

"More?" I kidded. "What more could there possibly be?"

Ayob, learning to be a "Walking Encyclopedia" from his grandfather, just laughed.

"Well, let's see," he said. "There is plenty more around Nazareth. And I think you might like Bethlehem. And you might like Jerusalem."

I laughed back. I could not wait.

I sat for a few moments and looked around. And I realized as much as Ein Karem, and the Church of the Visitation was mostly about Mary and Elizabeth, it was also about John the Baptist. This would have been where he was born and raised. And next to the Church of the Visitation was the Church of John the Baptist, built over the grotto where he was believed born. Excavations near the church discovered fragments dating to the 5th century.

And just down the street was St. Joseph's Church. Tradition says it was originally built over the Holy family's workshop, where Joseph did his carpentry. I overheard another tour guide talking about a cave underneath the church, typical where people would have lived in first century Galilee. Today's St. Joseph's Church is a modern, simple building, surrounded by ancient rocks. Here is where Jesus would have grown up as a child.

I paused and thought about Mary. And then Elizabeth. And then John the Baptist. And then Joseph. And then Jesus. Everything was happening right where I was.

Ayob walked by me again.

"Still okay, Bob?" he asked, smiling.

I could only nod my head.

Ein Karem - Church of the Visitation

"It is okay," he said. "This place gets to everybody."

We had some time to browse and shop. I walked past a restaurant called Pundak Ein Karem. A woman outside waved me in.

"Liver Pate special!"

I couldn't help but laugh. Not a dish in the world could appeal to me less than liver pate. I shook my head at her. I walked up to her and introduced myself.

"My name is Bob," I said. "I am writing about Ein Karem. But no liver pate!"

She laughed.

"My name is Salah," she said. "What does Mr. Bob like to eat?"

It was already hot outside. I needed something light.

"Ice cream?" I inquired.

Salah laughed and pointed down the street.

"Golda's," she said. "Mr. Bob go to Golda's"

I felt like I could not let her down, so I headed down the street to find Golda's. I did not have to look far. Tourists were lined up down the street. I waited about 15 minutes to get to the counter. The first selection I saw was potato chip ice cream. Not for me, but better than liver pate ice cream.

I quickly began looking for something less radical, like say, vanilla or chocolate. I settled on something called banana date.

It went down just fine.

"In a loud voice she exclaimed: "Blessed are you among women, and blessed is the child you will bear! But what am I so favored, that the mother of my Lord should come to me? As soon as the sound of your greeting reached my ears, the baby in my womb leaped for joy. Blessed is she who has believed that the Lord would fulfill his promises to her."

CHAPTER 8

Bethlehem

*"O little town of Bethlehem, how still we see thee lie!
Above thy deep and dreamless sleep the silent stars go by.
Yet in thy dark streets shineth the everlasting Light;
The hopes and fears of all the years are met in thee tonight."*

The famous Delores "with a K" Khouri

Bethlehem

I asked many of the tourists in our group what they wanted to see most on our journey, where they wanted to go, and what they grew up dreaming about when they thought of the Holy Land. For many of them, rightly so, it was Jerusalem, to be in the Garden of Gethsemane where Jesus prayed, to walk with the cross up to Calvary, and to kneel at the empty tomb. For others it was the preachings around Nazareth, to walk in the Sea of Galilee where Jesus made fishers of men, or to be baptized in the Jordan River, as Jesus was by John the Baptist. I listened intently as others, like me, knew their prized moments were at hand.

"The highlight of my life," said Delores Koury, who was approaching 90 years old. "I am not sure how I am going to handle all of this. What a thrill. I am so glad I am here for this."

We sat and talked. "That's Koury with a K," she told me firmly. "All of the other Couri's on this trip are Couri's with a C."

"Why is that?" I asked.

"Because Bob," she smiled. "I am special."

For me, my special place was always Bethlehem, tucked in the Judean Hills. The other sites would be incredible and life changing. But for me, It was always going to be Bethlehem.

"Away in a manger, no crib for a bed, the little Lord Jesus lay down his sweet head......"

My faith always takes me back to that night Luke told us about. I close my eyes and I see Mary and Joseph, a donkey, and no room at the Inn. I see a step back into the centuries, a quiet little town. And it is that night, always that night.

"The stars in the sky look down where he lay, the little Lord Jesus asleep on the hay......"

I close my eyes again and I see shepherd's in the fields, a star overhead, and a voice from above. I see it crystal clear. In my heart, the birth of my Lord and Savior rules any other moment I can close my eyes and see.

Bethlehem was not just the birthplace of our Messiah, but also the home of Ruth and Boaz, and the birthplace of Kings Saul and David.

And now here I was. Sadly, I soon discovered my dreams of biblical Bethlehem would bear little resemblance to the city that stood before me today, where as Palestinian flag flew above the city.

I found a city not quiet and quaint, but as commercialized as any other. Streets are long, winding and narrow, littered with souvenir shops hawking olive wood carvings, craft stores, and small restaurants. You can smell the freshly baked bread in the air. Houses are stone mason. There are murals and street art displayed around town. Tourist buses and cars jam the streets. On Manger Street we passed Stars and Bucks and KFC. Further down was a tattoo shop. We passed the market area, which seemed to lack character.

Bethlehem today has a population of about 30,000, and it appeared as if most of them were gathered right in front of me. Tourists were flocking into and out of churches as our bus slowly crept through the streets.

A crying baby in a little manger seemed a million miles away. Whatever I had pictured in my mind, and sang about on Christmas eve, would have to stay locked in my mind.

In the 1970's, a large number of Christians called Bethlehem home. The area around the city and nearby small villages was about 90% Christian. By the 1980's, the Christian population dipped to around 80%, and at that time, Bethlehem was placed under Palestinian Authority, a Fatah controlled government exercising civil control over much of the West Bank area. That means there is military rule over the area, with travel permits being rarely issued to Bethlehem residents.

Today, a large wall surrounds parts of Bethlehem, called the West Bank Barrier, separating Bethlehem from the rest of Israel. The wall is covered with graffiti from one end to the other. The city has one of the highest rates of unemployment in the West Bank, yet its price of land has skyrocketed in recent years.

All of this has put many people living in Bethlehem under difficult lives. Many have fled. And today, the number of Christians living in Bethlehem is down to nearly 10%, with Muslims taking over the area.

Simply put, the Bethlehem that was once a thriving Christian community today is a watered down version of itself, among the poorest cities in the Palestinian Territories. And worse, the fear is that the Christian tradition is disappearing.

Before leaving for the Holy Land, I had made arrangements to meet some locals at Beit Sahour Community Center, just down the street from the Beit Sahour Souvenir Store.

I wanted to learn about their land, their history, and their faith. What I got was an earful of frustration, angry that Israeli settlements now surround their city, with a wall separating them from the more vibrant Jerusalem.

"There is an ISIS influence here," an older man who said he has lived his entire life here told me. "Bethlehem is not the same town I grew up in.

Things are much different today. It is like we live in a prison. Guards with guns at the wall."

I told the men I understood, but reminded them that the area had always been under some sort of occupation, from the Babylonians to the British Mandate. When Jesus was born, I reminded them, Bethlehem would have been under Roman rule, and life may have been much worse.

"Yes, but it is not just in Bethlehem," another man told me. "It is happening everywhere. Look at Gaza. Thousands of Christians were living there. Then Hamas took over. Good luck finding Christians there today."

A younger man from the group had pretty much accepted his fate. "We are suffocating here. We are used to the occupation by now. We do not like it, but it is what it is. You adapt. Israel controls everything. Sometimes the water is good. Sometimes it is bad. Same for the sewage. And most of the time, we are made to feel like we are second class citizens."

"You just know they do not want us here," another man said. "They are pushing us out. They want to isolate us from Jerusalem and our history."

"People are afraid of living in an Islamic State," another said. "If they have the chance to leave, they leave. Some of us do not have that chance. You never know when there will be a war. Nobody wants that for their children, so they leave."

As I thanked the group and said goodbye, one of them shook my hand hard, looked me in the eye and asked a question I could not bear answering.

"What will happen to Bethlehem when there are no more Christians here? Imagine a life in the land of Jesus without Christians. Who is going to take care of our Holy Sites? This is also where David was born. Rachel's tomb is here."

The man paused.

"What will happen to our churches? What will happen to the place where Jesus was born?"

I nodded that I understood his grief. I told him that it would be my grief too. The man smiled.

"You see that wall that now surrounds our city?" he asked me. "We are not even able to go into Jerusalem. Many of our people have never been there. How would Mary and Joseph be able to get here from Nazareth if they ran into that eight foot wall?"

I paused.

"To me," I told the men, "your city, Bethlehem, is the center of the world. It means everything to me. That will never change, no matter how much the world changes. People who seek Jesus will always seek Bethlehem."

The men nodded and smiled. As I left, one of them said something that stuck with me. "There is an understanding here, despite the difficulties and despite the different religions. Jews, Muslims and Christians all understand the importance of this area. We are all doing our best to preserve it."

That would seem to be a start, I thought.

I ventured back out into the streets, sad that Bethlehem was not what I had pictured. But I saw a sign proclaiming the "Prince of Peace," and I no longer cared. Yes, I would remember the modern version of Bethlehem. But in my mind and memory, and in my heart and dreams, it would always be my special version, with a baby in a manger.

"For Christ is born of Mary
And gathered all above
While mortals sleep, the angels keep
Their watch of wondering love
O morning stars together
Proclaim thy holy birth
And praises sing to God the King
And peace to men on earth."

CHAPTER 9

The Shepherds' Field

"And there were shepherds living out in the fields nearby, keeping watch over their flocks at night. An angel of the Lord appeared to them, and the glory of the Lord shone around them, and they were terrified. But the angel said to them, "Do not be afraid. I bring you good news that will cause great joy for all the people. Today in the town of David a Savior has been born to you; he is the Messiah, the Lord. This will be a sign to you: You will find a baby wrapped in cloths and lying in a manger. Suddenly a great company of the heavenly host appeared with the angel, praising God and saying. Glory to God in the highest heaven, and on earth peace to those on whom his favor rests."

That night. If I could only go back in time, just once, to any night in the history of the world, it would be that night. And if I could go back to any place, it would be the place where I was now standing, in an empty field, staring at the sky, imagining what a night looked like 2,000 years ago. Because on that glorious night, about 500 people lived in the area around Bethlehem. There were shepherd's working in the field where I stood tending their flock. Their goal was to raise their sheep without any blemishes, so they could be sacrificed in the temple in Jerusalem. The shepherd's would bring their sheep in at night as it was too dangerous to leave them outside among nature's predators. But on this night the shepherd's did not bother with the sheep. On this night, they were called by God. I still find it humbling that it was the

Destination: Holy Land

"A Savior has been born to you"

shepherd's who received the message from the heavens. These were men who were considered "unclean," and were banned from entering any temple to worship. They were considered the lowest of all people in rank of importance. They held jobs nobody wanted. They were uneducated, low class outcasts.

They were nobody. How fitting that God chose them.

"Blessed are the meek, for they shall inherit the earth."

This was another Bible story deeply etched in my mind from childhood. I close my eyes, and picture what I have pictured a thousand times. This was a place I had to see, and I had to see it alone, on my terms. This is the area where Jacob settled some 4,000 years ago. Urbanization has obviously changed the land over the centuries. And although I could see rolling hills with brown and dry fields in front of me, it became difficult to picture where the shepherd's may have been on that glorious night. Two hillsides led to a ravine. In the distance you could still see caves, "where the shepherd's watched over their flock."

Our tourist group soon realized there were times that I disappeared from them, either to talk with locals, sample some cuisine, or more frequently, to have a few minutes alone with my thoughts. The Shepherd's Field, just a couple of miles east of Bethlehem, was one of them. I waved to one of the people I was touring with. "Don't leave without me," I hollered. I knew they wouldn't, because by this point they always wondered where I went and what I found. Today, I would find peace, solitude, and talk to God.

I needed to find my spot. I reached into my pocket to find the piece of scrap paper, where I had written the words of Luke. The angels were gone now, and the shepherd's were talking to one another.

"Let us now go even unto Bethlehem, and see this thing which is come to pass, which the Lord hath made known unto us."

I walked over to where my best guess was to where the shepherd's may have been tending their flock that night. I had researched the area, and knew I needed to be just east of the Church of the Nativity, and about two miles east of Bethlehem. I knew I was close, I chose my spot, and did what I planned on doing once I knew I was coming to the Holy Land. I looked back west over the hills, toward Bethlehem. Then I knelt down, looked up, and gazed into the sky. I put my headphones on, hit play, and closed my eyes.

> "......Angels we have heard on high
> Sweetly singing o'er the plains,
> And the mountains in reply
> Echoing their joyous strains.
> Gloria, in excelsis Deo! Gloria in excelsis Deo!......"

This was me with God. It was as raw as it could possibly be. Whatever I wanted to say, I needed to say right now. The most important thing in my life is my personal relationship with God. You can read your devotionals in the morning, and you can pray at night. But walking with God on your shoulder, whispering in your ear, having a conversation in the quietest moments, that's where I meet God, and that is where I needed to meet him now.

It was daylight and not dark. There was not a shepherd or sheep to be found. I looked in every direction and could only see a field. And then I sat, and then we talked, just like other talks all the time.

> ".....Here I am, Lord. Is it I, Lord? I have heard You calling in the night. I will go, Lord. If You lead me. I will hold Your people in my heart....."

And then a gust of wind blew. Hard. I grabbed my hat and smiled. He's got me. He's always got me. Simply, it was another incredible moment on my journey, that I knew had many more to come.

Destination: Holy Land

After I said what I needed to say, I slowly got up, and walked back to find the others at the Shepherd's Field site. There is an arch overhead at the entrance that says " Gloria in excelsis Deo." There is a cave by the field that has an altar for prayer where I saw many from our group. As you step down into the cave, there is a mosaic, again with this on the wall: "Gloria in excelsis Deo." The words of the angels are inscribed in gold. The cave itself is now enclosed. You keep walking and discover that there are actually two sites dedicated to the Shepherd's Field. A worker at the chapel saw me taking notes and approached me. I asked him about the history.

"We have found remnants here from the first century," he told me. I nodded, looked around, and asked about the other churches nearby.

"Fourth of fifth century," he said. "Built over many times."

The new church was built 50 years ago, adjacent to the cave, he said. The original church was in a cave, and the new church still has some of the old remains. At the front of the chapel a large angel looms just above the entrance. Inside the church three large paintings hang, telling of the shepherd's journey on that holy night. The first shows an angel hovering over three shepherd's who are sitting by their flock; the second shows the shepherd's visiting the newborn king; the third shows the shepherd's celebrating Jesus' birth. And then you notice it….the light. It appears to break through the windows.

As I was looking upward, I heard the soothing voice of the Walking Encyclopedia.

"It is meant to represent the light of the angels when they appeared to the shepherd's," said Anton, smiling at me as always, knowing the teacher knew much more than the student.

"This place……" I slowly began.

"This place," he said, "is 4,000 years old."

"Jacob," I said quietly.

"The shepherd's," Anton said.

We looked at each other. I knew that what everything meant to me also meant to him.

"We leave in ten minutes," he said. "I get to come back next week. This is your only chance. Do what you have to do."

I nodded and went back outside one more time to look around. I walked back to my spot. I Looked up to the heavens one last time. I knelt down on my knees one last time. And one last time, I put on my headphones and hit play.

The Shepherds' Field

> "…..Come to Bethlehem and see
> Him whose birth the angels sing;
> Come, adore on bended knee
> Christ the Lord, the newborn King.
> Gloria in excelsis Deo.
> Gloria in excelsis Deo……."

I could tell you what that moment meant to me. But by now, if you have made it this far, I think you know. And guess what is next?

"When the angels had left them and gone into heaven, the shepherds said to one another, "Let's go to Bethlehem and see this thing that has happened, which the Lord has told us about." So they hurried off and found Mary and Joseph, and the baby, who was lying in the manger. When they had seen him, they spread the word concerning what had been told them about this child, and all who heard it were amazed at what the shepherds said to them."

CHAPTER 10

Basilica of the Nativity

"So Joseph also went up from the town of Nazareth in Galilee to Judea, to Bethlehem the town of David, because he belonged to the house and line of David. He went there to register with Mary, who was pledged to be married to him and was expecting a child. While they were there, the time came for the baby to be born, and she gave birth to her first-born, a son. She wrapped him in cloths and placed him in a manger, because there was no guest room available for them."

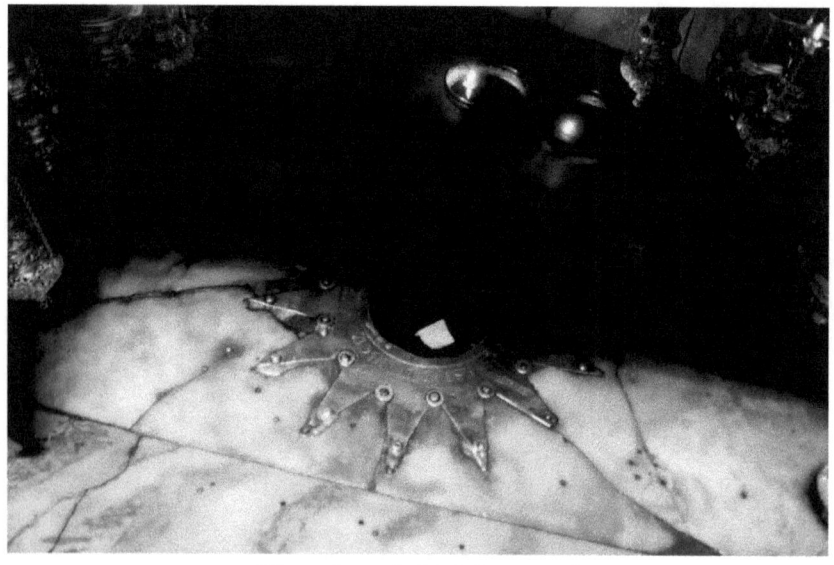

"Two minutes behind the curtain"

Basilica of the Nativity

I slowly walked toward the Basilica of the Nativity, weaving my way past Manger Square, Bethlehem's busiest spot, and then through a large courtyard in front of the church.

"We have got this Bob," said Diana Joseph as she grabbed my arm to go inside. "Right?"

I nodded as best as I could, but in my heart I knew better. You do not prepare for this moment in time. Joseph was with a group from Peoria, Illinois that had taken it upon themselves to watch over me.

"We came here for this," she told me. "This. Right here, right now. This is our time with Jesus."

She squeezed my arm. We kept moving forward, in silence, among hundreds of tourists.

"We got this, right?" I whispered back as we entered.

The first thing you notice upon entering the Basilica is how dark it is. There is a mysterious feel to it. It is cool inside. You look around and realize there are no pews. The interior of the church is bare. There are five aisles, separated by four columns of pillars. When you watch Christmas Eve services from Bethlehem, you are watching them from the Basilica of the Nativity.

This is the oldest major church in the Holy Land. We have written references to the Nativity cave that date to 160 AD. Pieces of the original floor still exist. The church that stands today is only the second church on site. A church was first built on this holy site in the year 339, then destroyed in the year 529 by the Samaritans. Christians rebuilt it, but In the year 614, the Persians invaded the area and destroyed all the Christian churches except this one, because mosaics on the churches facade portrayed the infant Jesus being worshiped by Persian holy men. Its last major repair was in the year 1480, and in the centuries that have passed, ancient artifacts have been found, from angels covered in plaster to the building's original doors.

And as historic as the church was, I came to see what was beneath the church's high altar: the Grotto of the Nativity.

The birthplace of baby Jesus, away in that manger, no crib for a bed.

As we entered the area, we were met with hundreds of worshipers who were there ahead of us. They were all trying to make their way to a small low door, the "Door of Humility" that would take them down to where Jesus was born. There were no lines. There was no organization. Just hundreds of people, young and old, trying to squeeze their way into that small door. We were twenty people wide, where eventually two people would make their way down the steps.

Time went by. We barely moved. It was hot inside. Two Muslim guards kept watch over the group. On this, the holiest of Christian sites, we were taking our orders from Muslims. There were no words to describe this.

"No talking," they would scream if they heard something. Every few minutes one of them would holler "no talking." I could see some people giving up in frustration or anger and leaving. Not me and Diana. We would be here until the end of time if necessary. I put my headphones back on and turned the Muslim guards off.

> "......O Holy night!
> The stars are brightly shining
> It is the night of our dear Savior's birth
> Long lay the world in sin and error pining
> Till He appeared and the soul felt its worth......."

We kept slowly inching our way forward. The temperature got hotter. I watched some elderly people fall. And then finally, we were there. A light shined over the very low "Door of Humility." I guessed the entrance to be about 4 feet high. Another Muslim guard stood at the entrance to this holiest of Christian sites. You had to step down narrow steep steps worn down over centuries by the feet of pilgrims trying to get into the grotto. It was dark and slippery heading down.

It did not matter. I was there.

Inside the grotto was a small, stuffy area. The walls were blackened by touch over time. Only a few of us were there now, waiting our turn. In front of us was a curtain, where two people at a time were entering as two others left.

"Two minutes," the guard told us. "You have two minutes behind the curtain."

I watched the first two people leave crying. Was I capable of holding myself together for two minutes? I decided I did not care.

A few more groups came out. It was incredible watching people walk in with smiles on their faces, and then walk out two minutes later filled with emotion.

And then it was my time.

There was an older man standing next to me. He looked up at me knowing fate had put the two of us together for this experience. I nodded and reached out my hand to his, and we walked under the curtain together.

The exact spot where Jesus was born is a 14 pointed silver star sitting on a marble floor, with the inscription "Hic De Virgine Maria Jesus Christus

Basilica of the Nativity

Natus," translated to "Here Jesus Christ was born to the Virgin Mary." In the middle of the star is a hole where you can reach down and touch a stone, believed to be the stone Mary laid Jesus on when he was born.

I looked at the man next to me, we squeezed our hands tightly, and we knelt on the floor.

And then for two minutes, I just cried. It was impossible not to. These weren't tears of sadness or tears of joy. They were just tears. I felt so small, so insignificant, so wondering how I stacked up in Jesus' eyes.

"Two minutes up," the guard shouted.

I looked at the man next to me. Tears were running down his face. We squeezed our hands again.

"My name is Bob," I told him.

"George," he said.

We stood up and walked out.

As I exited the grotto, I turned my headphones back on.

> "......*A thrill of hope the weary world rejoices*
> *For yonder breaks a new and glorious morn*
> *Fall on your knees; O hear the Angel voices*
> *O night divine, O night when Christ was born....*"

I fought my way back through the massive crowd of people still waiting to get into the grotto. Finally, I found the church's entrance and headed outside. I found a place to sit and contemplate what had just happened.

My mind was both buzzing, and blank. Where do you go from here? How does anything the rest of my life compare to this?

I felt a tap on my shoulder and looked up. It was Diana.

"We did it Bob!" she said.

I saw tears in her eyes.

"How do we ever explain this?" she asked.

I thought about it. People will ask what it was like. I will try to write about it. I will not be able to.

"I will just tell them I cried," I told her. "For two minutes, I knelt there and I cried."

We soon caught up with the others from our group. Unlike our other stops, there was little banter or discussion about what we had just gone through. We all had the same experience. Emotions were raw. As we exited the Basilica, I looked frantically one last time for George, but never saw him in the masses of people.

Destination: Holy Land

The bus ride back was more of the same. Eerily quiet, nearly 100 tourists contemplating what they had just experienced. I looked out the window and went back to my headphones.

> "......Truly He taught us to love one another
> His law is love and His gospel is peace
> Chains He shall break
> For the slave is our brother
> And in His Name
> All oppression shall cease……."

In my heart, I know Jesus was born to save the world, a gift from God. And no matter what my problems are, he gives me hope to overcome anything. But today, I did not have the strength to kneel at his birthplace without crying profusely. Somehow, I see him smiling down at me, chuckling, and telling me it is all right.

I was certainly not alone.

> *"But you, Bethlehem, in the land of Judah,*
> * are by no means least among the rulers of Judah;*
> *for out of you will come a ruler*
> * who will shepherd my people Israel."*

CHAPTER 11

Milk Grotto

"And after the wise men departed, behold an angel of the Lord appeared in sleep to Joseph, saying Arise, and take the child and his mother and fly into Egypt: and be there until I shall tell thee. For it will come to pass that Herod will seek the child to destroy him."

"Go Bonolo!"

"Please visit my husband. Please visit my children."

I heard the chanting and cheering in the distance as I walked up to the Milk Grotto, the site where Joseph, Mary and Jesus fled to and found refuge from Herod before fleeing into Egypt. The "milk grotto" name comes from the story that a single drop of milk from Mary as she was breast feeding baby Jesus, spilled beneath her onto the floor of the cave, and changed the stone's color from red to white.

"Please visit my husband. Please visit my children," got louder and louder as our group got closer to the site.

Once there, I saw a woman dancing and singing. Friends were at her side, singing and clapping, with her. They were all wearing beautiful multi-colored African outfits. I walked closer.

"Go Bonolo!" I heard a man holler.

I looked at a tourist next to me. Her name tag said Bonnie from Dallas.

"What is happening here?" I asked her.

"New mothers come here praying for a miracle so they can become pregnant," she said. "They are unable to conceive for one reason or another, so they come to the grotto from all over the world to pray to Mary to bring them a baby."

I looked confused.

"There is white chalk down in the grotto below the church. They believe if you mix the chalk with your water and food, and pray to Mary, you will be blessed and have a child."

I looked again at Bonolo who was still dancing and singing.

"She is praying to get pregnant," the woman told me. "That is why she is chanting 'please visit my husband'. It sounds like there might be a problem with his fertility."

I left Bonolo and headed toward the chapel. The street was filled with small shops selling olive wood carvings. They were trying to catch as many of the tourists as possible who had made the short walk from the Basilica of the Nativity just down the street toward the grotto. I stopped for a moment to look around. It was impossible to differentiate any of the gift shops from each other. Wooden crosses, last supper pictures, figurines of Mary.

We entered the church site that was built above the grotto in the 5th century. There is a beautiful mosaic in the courtyard that dates to that time period. The present chapel was built in the 1800's. A statue of the Virgin Mary breastfeeding baby Jesus sits just above the grotto entrance. There is a crowd gathered around the statue, as visitors are kneeling and praying

Milk Grotto

at Mary's feet. I walked inside where it was both cool and quiet, and sat in a pew in the back. I looked to the end of the church where there was a modern part of the chapel, with a sign asking everyone to be quiet.

I quietly asked an usher why the church needed the sign.

"It is for the nuns," he said. "Look, they keep a constant vigil, praying for peace."

I watched for a few minutes, saw a group of nuns get up, only to be replaced by others who began quietly praying. It was like a changing of the guard.

"This goes on all day?" I asked the usher.

He nodded his head.

I walked my way through the church. I saw both Christian and Muslim visitors. At the altar I watched as Muslims women took turns lighting candles. It was heartwarming.

As you head downward the steps leading down into the grotto, you notice the white, chalkish rock formations. The grotto itself is very small, with three separate caves. There are white decorations engraved in the walls. Once inside, you see a painting of the Virgin Mary as she is nursing baby Jesus. Again, you come across more people kneeling and praying.

I found myself standing next to one of the Franciscan nuns, and said hello. Her name was Naomi.

"Who runs the church and grotto?" I asked.

"We do," she smiled and told me.

I told her about the woman I saw dancing outside.

"We have heard from thousands of families who have had miracle babies born after they had visited us," she said. "And not just Christians. Muslim and Israeli families too."

She watched me smile and nod.

"It is about faith and belief," she said. "It is Christianity at its core."

I asked her about the story of the grotto turning from red to white. She smiled again.

"All of the other grotto's throughout the area are the same color....red. Something incredible had to happen to turn this one to white."

"Amazing," I said.

"Come, follow me," she said and led me back upstairs, where I saw a group of people jamming into a small room at the right side of the exit of the church.

"Go on," she said. "You will find what you are looking for in there."

I worked my way inside, to discover a huge wall with letters and pictures sent from people all over the world who had traveled earlier to the milk grotto to pray for babies. Their stories were heartbreaking. Their faith was amazing.

There are hundreds of letters on the wall, testimonies from people all over the world, retelling their stories of being unable to conceive, of visiting the grotto and praying to Mary, and then having a miraculous baby. I see letters from Brazil, from Poland, from New Zealand, and of course, from across America.

And then you see them. People jammed around the wall, staring at photographs. Photographs of those same parents, from every corner of the world, now holding their miracle babies. It was a stunning testimonial.

I walked back to the church entrance where the sun was waiting for me, along with the Franciscan nun.

"Well?" she asked, smiling again.

I smiled back. "Well, I already have three adult children. I do not need anymore, so I don't think I will be sending my wife here!"

She laughed out loud. "Be safe. Walk with God," she told me.

"I will," I said. "Thank you Sister."

I left the church and our group began to head toward our buses. As we did, I heard the chants and noticed Bonolo was still dancing. I wondered how long she had been there, and how long she might stay. I looked at her group of supporters and wandered over.

"Hello," I said to one man holding out my hand, hoping he could understand me. "My name is Bob."

"Hello Bob," he said in broken English as we shook hands.

"Tell me about Bonolo," I asked.

"She cannot have a baby," he told me. "We came to pray to Mary to have a baby."

"I hope it works," I told him, telling him I was writing a book, and I asked for his name.

"Thank you Bob," he said. "My name is Sibusiso."

I watched as Bonolo kept dancing, and the crowd kept cheering.

"Baby for Bonolo!" they cried. And then "Hear us Mary!"

After a few minutes, another nun came out and approached the group.

"Give this to Bonolo," she told them.

I got closer and realized it was a milk mixture from the limestone rock of the church, a far cry from the Prairie Farms gallon jug at home.

Milk Grotto

"We have the milk! We have the milk!" the group shouted.

Bonolo danced her way closer to the milk, as Sibusiso led me toward her. I watched as a woman with her poured the milk pocket into some water, and over a banana, then gave it to Bonolo as the crowd cheered her on. She ate and drank, then fell to her knees and everyone began praying together.

"Hear us Mary! Hear us Mary! Please bring a child to Bonolo and husband!"

And then she began dancing again.

I asked Sibusiso if Bonolo's husband was here. He was not.

"How long will you stay?" I asked him.

"I guess until she stops dancing," he said.

It was getting warm now. The afternoon heat was setting in.

"How long has she been dancing so far?" I wondered.

"We got here when the sun came up."

All I could do was look at her and shake my head. What incredible belief.

I shook hands with Sibusiso and began to leave. As I walked past Bonolo and her group I paused and chanted with them.

"Please visit my husband. Please visit my children."

"So he got up, took the child and his mother during the night and left for Egypt, where he stayed until the death of Herod. And so was fulfilled what the Lord had said through the prophet:
"Out of Egypt I called my son."

CHAPTER 12

Nazareth

"Philip found Nathanael and told him, "We have found the One Moses wrote about in the Law, the One the prophets foretold—Jesus of Nazareth, the son of Joseph." "Can anything good come from Nazareth?" Nathaniel asked. "Come and see," said Philip."

I knew that much of any Holy Land journey will be centered around the historic city of Nazareth, where Jesus grew up and taught in nearby cities. Today Nazareth is Israel's largest Arab community with a much smaller number of Christian residents. There are very few Jews living here anymore.

For Christians, what really matters is this is where a young virgin girl said 'yes' and changed the course of history.

Before heading out on our first stop, there was breakfast waiting for the group.. The buffet menu throughout the day consisted of stuffed grape leaves with tzatziki, hummus with shiitake mushrooms, fatayer, kubeh filled with mutton, zucchini sheikh al-mahshi with white rice and yogurt, and focaccia with smoked goose breast.

Egg McMuffin's were down the street nearby if you felt the need to sneak away. You might not find Starbucks, but Squarebucks will do.

Other tourists saw my pen and notebook and stopped by to inquire.

"You are writing a book?" asked Rita Elojail. She grew up in Lebanon, and now lived in New York.

"I am," I said. "My bucket list."

"This is a dream come true for me," she said. "I grew up in Lebanon, but we were never allowed to come to the Holy Land. I have been wanting to come here my whole life. It was always in the back of my mind. I knew I was always going to come here someday."

"Me too," I told her. "Me too."

Rita and I shared a background in journalism, hers in Lebanon.

"But nothing has prepared me for this," she said.

I glanced at her plate filled with the hummus and mushrooms. She smiled and looked at mine.

"One little egg, Bob?"

"Special order, just for me," I laughed.

Rita was tall and wore a baseball cap. I told her I would look for her whenever I got lost.

As we prepared to get on the bus for the day, another woman spotted me.

"They say you are writing about our trip," she said.

"Yes ma'am," I said. "I am."

"My name is Fadia," she said, holding out her hand. "Fadia Voutros. I flew from Houston. This is so important to me. I needed to make this trip once in my life, and I am not getting any younger."

I smiled and we laughed. "Neither am I," I said.

"This is my calling," she said as she grabbed my arm. "It was now or never."

"Houston?" I wondered. "It is going to be a hot one today. It should feel just like home to you."

Fadia laughed. "I didn't think anyplace could be worse than Houston. I may have traveled around the world to find it."

If your mind pictures Nazareth as going back in time, to a deserted desert, a rustic old city, with donkeys and farm animals aplenty, you will be sadly mistaken. Traffic, while moving is an absolute mess. If there are rules of the road here, nobody has read them. What would be considered road rage in America seems to happen every few minutes on crowded highways here. You will not need that car if you are driving around in town. That is because the streets are too narrow to drive in. If you are walking in a street, and a car is coming toward you, the only option is to head to the wall.

Those city streets have no names, which is a boom to the tour guides. Nazareth itself is spread out, but the holy sights within the city are all easily within walking distance. I heard much more Arabic language being spoken as I walked the streets, and everyone was friendly to all the American tourists. If there was tension between any of the religions here, it never showed its face.

I soon discovered a strange feel: I was in a Muslim city, set in a Jewish state, with a Christian legacy. I wondered who lived here today, and why? What was their life like? They would have to juggle with social, economic, religious and cultural concerns.

I inquired of one of the pastors on our trip.

"Christians who make the decision to live here understand they must deal with the environment around them," he said. "Most of them obviously support Israel. But they have to keep it to themselves because they know they live in a large anti-Israeli Muslim area."

As you navigate your way around Nazareth, and the neighboring cities where Jesus preached, the stark reality of the geography gives one pause. For example, the distance between Nazareth and Jerusalem, a journey Jesus and his followers took many times, is nearly 100 miles. Imagine how long those hikes would have taken if they were even walking five miles per hour. They were not wearing Skechers back in the day. The travel was difficult today by tour bus. Two thousand years ago?

The city itself is divided into two parts, 'The Old City' and 'The New City.' For our journey with Jesus, we would immerse ourselves in 'The Old City.' And when you step into it, you will see tour buses and tour groups from every corner of the world. Within minutes, I crossed paths with a group from Ethiopia, and then bowed with a group from Japan. And you realize they are there for the same reason you are.

It is their bucket list. For some, it was now or never.

Today Nazareth has the feel of a small, diverse, poor town. Buildings are constructed mostly with stone. More than half of all Arab households here live in poverty. There is certainly nothing fancy here. Small mom and pop merchants line the streets, all selling the same merchandise, desperately hollering at tourists as they pass by. The headscarves, sandals and pomegranates that you bypass will be available again in 30 seconds down the street. Without the holy sites and Christian tourists, it would resemble many American towns that got bypassed by highways, and were left to die.

In the time of Jesus, Nazareth was widely considered a wicked place, a tiny, unspectacular agricultural village, a mere stopping spot for Roman soldiers passing through to head someplace much more important. Indeed, a Godless place, where nothing good ever came from.

"Can anything good come from Nazareth?" Nathaniel asked.

And yet Nazareth gave the world Mary, and then gave us our Lord and Savior.

Nazareth

When Gabriel visited Mary, Nazareth at the time would have probably had less than 500 residents. There was a synagogue, as its remains have been uncovered. And yet today, despite its world famous name, it only has about 75,000 residents, roughly the same size as Hammond, Indiana or Dothan, Alabama. Buried underneath today's 'Old City' of Nazareth, long lost to history, wars, and weather, is the time of Jesus.

One can surmise that Nazareth is still on the map today only because of its most famous resident.

As we toured the city, I wondered what Jesus would have seen 2,000 years ago. Had he looked south into the Jezreel Valley, he would have seen Biblical history. There was Gideon and Saul, Josiah and Ahab, Barack and Deborah. We know he worked in Nazareth as a carpenter with Joseph. I pondered what life must have been like there for him in Nazareth after he lost his father. He was the big brother now, to James, Joseph, Simon and Juda, plus two sisters. He would be the leader of the family now. The teacher who always talked about comforting, about helping those who were hurting.

We know nothing about Jesus life from age 12-30. I doubt he walked around in those times calling himself the Messiah. He had to be pushed into that role years later in Cana by Mary. But for some reason he left Nazareth and headed to Capernaum, and the rest is history. And when he eventually returns to his hometown, he is lucky to escape alive.

"Truly I tell you, no prophet is accepted in his hometown," he tells his old friends.

The Nazarene's responded by driving him from the synagogue, marching him to the edge of a cliff.

While my group was celebrating their daily mass, I made my way to Nazareth Village, an open air museum set up to resemble the time of Jesus. It was not part of our itinerary. I jumped into a tour group and raised my hand. A guide named Daniel called on me.

"That cliff," I began. "Any idea where that cliff might have been?"

Daniel smiled and waved his hands at the hills.

"If we only knew. We have cliffs everywhere."

I looked around at all the hills. And I remembered how that night, 2,000 ago, ended, on the edge of that cliff.

Jesus turned, faced his detractors, and calmly walked away.

The Prince of Peace. My Savior.

Destination: Holy Land

"And when they had performed all things according to the law of the Lord, they returned into Galilee, to their own city Nazareth."

CHAPTER 13

The Jordan River

"Jesus came from Galilee. He went to John at the Jordan River to be baptized by him. John tried to stop Him. He said, 'I need to be baptized by You. Do You come to me?' Jesus said to him, 'Let it be done now. We should do what is right.' John agreed and baptized Jesus."

"A loser to Mother Nature, and to man."

Destination: Holy Land

As our United Dreamliner flew, for hour after hour over the darkness of the Atlantic Ocean, I tried to sleep, but could not. I tried to read, but could not. I tried to watch a movie, but could not. In the middle of the night, all I could do was stare out the window, and think.

For some reason, my mind drifted to scenes from some of my favorite movies. Dorothy stepping into the world of Oz in technicolor; Rocky running up all those steps in Philly, dancing with his arms raised; Cool Hand Luke swallowing 50 hard boiled eggs in one hour; Brando making a man an offer he could not refuse; De Niro blasting his way out of that Vietnam swamp cage; The real Holocaust survivors coming down the hill, one after another, at the end of *Schindler's List*.

But most of all, I thought about the opening scene of "The Gospel of John." First came the words: "In the beginning there was the Word, and the Word was with God, and the Word was God…….." And then a giant shadow appears, followed by a man walking along the sand in sandals.

It was Jesus walking to the Jordan River, where he would be baptized by John the Baptist. And I was heading to the Jordan River, where all I could think about as I stared into space was that I wanted to be baptized where Jesus was baptized. That thought kept me company at 40,000 feet in the middle of the night.

"Look, the Lamb of God, who takes away the sin of the world!" kept going through my mind at 600 miles per hour. But the Jordan went back further than Jesus. This after all was the barrier between Abraham and Lot's land. You find the Jordan River in the stories of both Moses and Joshua. This is where for years, after wandering the desert, Israelites crossed the river on dry ground after the flow of water was stopped for them.

This is where the world was introduced to Christianity. Certainly one of the holiest sites on earth.

Sadly, it was not to be, as my expectations of the Jordan River, the source of all holy water in Christianity, did not meet the reality of what our group discovered on the ground. In this case, Hollywood let me down.

"For those of you hoping to be baptized in the Jordan River, there are too many risks with that," one of the Catholic priests from Los Angeles told our group ahead of time. "You will see what I mean when we get there."

The tour this day began in Jericho, one of the oldest cities in the world, and where the Israeli's crossed the Jordan River to enter the Promised Land sometime around 1500 BC. Our bus pulled into the lower end of the Jordan,

The Jordan River

not far from Jericho, where it meets up with the Dead Sea. And the priest was right.

There is still a river, stretching more than 220 miles long with winding turns, not very large but very deep in spots. It is still both "the most crooked river in the world," and "the lowest river in the world." When the Jordan feeds into the Dead Sea, the depths reach some 1,300 feet.

But the Jordan River today barely resembles the river where John the Baptist would have baptized Jesus and John the disciple would have documented it 2,000 years ago. Today, the Jordan is nothing more than a stream, its flow nearly non-existent.

"About one tenth of what it was even 50 years ago," said our "Walking Encyclopedia," Anton. "A loser to Mother Nature, and to man."

Climate change has done its damage, but so too has man. You notice the smell immediately, and see the bugs in the air. There is a small sign by the shore that says "the water isn't potable."

Not exactly what dreams are made of.

None of that would have bothered me though. I just wanted to be baptized again, just as Jesus was. I would have settled for a bucket of water.

But not today. Not with raw sewage muddling the water along its banks. Sadly, the Jordan was nothing but a polluted mess, with a color that resembled sand.

"Heartbreaking," one of the women on our bus said. "Not at all what I expected. This was going to be the highlight of my trip."

Ah, Hollywood.

We followed Anton as he walked along the river.

"Water buffaloes used to roam in this area," Anton said.

"There is a dam called the Alumot Dam that is just to the north of us," Anton told the group. "It is south of the Sea of Galilee. Sadly, people keep dumping trash at the dam, and then it flows down the river to the lower level."

We made our way to a highway bridge overlooking the river, and the view was spectacular, betraying what lay below. You look down and realize what the Jordan meant not just to Christians, but also Muslims and Jews.

The river has also been affected over time by agricultural chemicals and local fish farms.

The lower end of the river where our tour group gathered was tiny, and it was hard to imagine the scene with Jesus and John the Baptist taking place anywhere near where the group was. I asked Anton where along the miles after miles of the winding river he thought the baptizing event might have occurred.

"Certainly not anywhere this far down near Jericho," he said. "Do you remember what happened the very next day after Jesus was baptized? That is your clue to the baptism site."

I did not know.

"What happened the next day," I wondered. "And where?"

Anton smiled, and in half Arabic, half English, and half something else, I made out the answer.

"The very next day after he was baptized, Jesus met Philip. And Philip lived in Bethsaida, which is on the north end of the Sea of Galilee. So the baptism had to happen way up there."

Of course, Anton knew much more.

"But where?" I asked.

"Probably in a place north called Yardenit," he said. "And people are still getting baptized up there on the northern end of the river. The further north you get, the cleaner the river is. The further south, where we are, the worse it gets."

I watched as others began looking up Yardenit on their phones.

"But some people claim the baptism took place near Al-Maghtas," Anton told the group, who quickly put their phones down. "That is on the eastern side of the Jordan."

Another mystery never to be answered. Either way, we were hundreds of miles away, not on the north or the east, but on the southern end. Nobody was being baptized today. Maybe next time.

Still, this was the Jordan River. This is where Jesus walked. This is where the gospel of John introduces him to the world. The river at my feet might now be a muddy swamp, but it would still mean so much to me. Two thousand years can take much away. But it can't take away Jesus, with John the Baptist, in that water, wherever it may be. And it didn't take away something else.

"Look over there at those plants," one of the tour pastors told our group. "The one's where the bees and bugs are gathering. Those plants are called yanbouts. They have been here forever. And what was John the Baptist eating? Locusts and wild honey."

And there was something else that Jesus and John the Baptist didn't see, and John did not witness 2,000 years ago: Today stood, a barbed wire fence, lined with armed soldiers, Jordanians on one side, Israelis on the other, stretching from Jordan to Israel. Where the river narrowed, they were close enough to see each other's eyes.

So sad.

As we left the river, I could hear other tourist's singing in the distance.

> "....As I went down in the river to pray,
> Studying about that good old way,
> And who shall wear the robe and crown,
> Good Lord show me the way!...."

Back on the bus I heard others talk about seeing some tourists wade in the water, but not get baptized. Some apparently filled water bottles to take back home. I had no interest in that.

I would rather have my dreams.

"As soon as Jesus was baptized, he went up out of the water. At that moment heaven was opened, and he saw the Spirit of God descending like a dove and alighting on him. And a voice from heaven said, "This is my Son, whom I love; with him I am well pleased."

CHAPTER 14

The Mount of Temptation

"Then Jesus was led by the Spirit into the wilderness to be tempted by the devil. After fasting forty days and forty nights, he was hungry. The tempter came to him and said, "If you are the Son of God, tell these stones to become bread." Jesus answered, "It is written: 'Man shall not live on bread alone, but on every word that comes from the mouth of God."

"All this I will give You if You will bow down and worship me"

The Mount of Temptation

The first thing I saw was a sign that said "The oldest city in the world. 10,000 years old. Temptation Mountain. Hisham Palace."

Our tour bus kept winding its way uphill, through twists and turns. I looked out the window and saw nothing but mountains, giant hills that just kept rolling, one after another after another.

Finally, the bus, barely moving up the steep inclines, came to a halt about halfway up the mountain..

"We cannot go any further," the guide announced. "The mountains are too steep."

Everyone on the bus looked at each other.

"Do not worry," the guide announced. "Shuttle cars will take us the rest of the way."

And then you realize, Jesus and his followers did not have a bus. They did not have a shuttle car.

Our destination was the Mount of Temptation, where Jesus fasted for 40 days and nights, and where he was tempted by Satan, who offered him rule over all the kingdoms of the world.

I walked from the bus to the shuttle car and looked around. The mountain was barren. Below me was the Judean Desert. We were overlooking the Jordan Valley. I could see the ancient city of Jericho in the distance. The stretch from there to Jerusalem would have been the area of the "Valley of the shadow of death" that David wrote about in Psalm 23.

Lolly Maroon, one of the travelers in my group, spotted me gawking.

"Come on Bob," she said. "Unless you want to walk the rest of the way."

"Not an option," I laughed, and we got in the car.

Like the bus, the shuttle car kept winding in circles heading uphill, mile after mile after mile.

I asked the driver how far up the mountain we were going.

"Over 1,000 feet," he said. "All in circles, just a few feet each time."

On the slopes of the mountain I could see the entrances to caves where people would have lived thousands of years ago.

We came up to a man and a woman who were walking up the road. Our driver offered them some water. I saw their backpacks and realized they were tourists.

"Hop in," I hollered. "We will make room."

They both shook their heads.

"Nope," the man said.

"Jesus did not ride in a shuttle," the woman hollered.

I could only nod in respect.

"How long have you been walking?" I asked them.

"About an hour," the man said. "Maybe you should join us."

I paused and looked outside. There was still a mountain in front of me. It was sweltering hot in the middle of a September day in the desert. The air conditioning in the car was very comforting.

"Maybe next time," I told them. And we sped off.

The car soon came to a stop. I thanked the driver and stepped out.

"Good luck," he said smiling.

Luck, I wondered? Why did I need luck?

Then I looked up and saw steps heading up to the top of the mountain. What appeared to be hundreds of steps. And I began the climb that Jesus made, albeit a tad shorter. About 15 minutes later, desperate for a break, I stopped and sat on a bench for a drink. A tour guide from another group passed me by.

"Sir," I hollered. "Excuse me. Any idea how much longer to get to the top?"

He looked at me and smiled. "We might be halfway. If you are lucky."

Halfway? How was I going to do this? Wait, Jesus did it for 40 days.

After a short rest and some water, I was ready to head back up the mountain. I passed some other people from my group who were resting along the way.

"Come on!" I hollered. "This is no big deal! You don't need to rest!"

Of course, they knew me by now, and they busted out laughing.

And then, finally, I arrived.

And the top was incredible.

There is a Monastery there that dates to 330 AD, making this one of the oldest monasteries in the Holy Land, just clinging to the curves on the mountain cliffs. Inside are sculptures of Jesus and Mary. There are crosses everywhere, and paintings on the ceiling. In the walls are cracks stuffed with small pieces of paper from visitors leaving prayer wishes.

A second, smaller Monastery nearby is built near a cave that has a stone they claim is the stone Jesus sat on during his fasting and temptation. Next to it is another cave called Quarantania, where Jesus is said to have rested while he fasted. There are other churches on the Mount, where other groups were reciting prayers outside.

The Mount of Temptation

I walked into the main Monastery and looked around. I only saw one monk there, sitting alone. Surely there had to be others. I walked around the area, and the other monasteries, but could find none.

Our group was gathering by the cliffs. It was time for the 'Walking Encyclopedia' to take over.

"We are standing about 400 meters above ground," Anton began. "This would also be the area where King David hid from Saul. This was also the location of King Herod's winter palace. This would have been a place for monks to hide if they feared persecution. There are 36 caves on the side of the mountain that the monks lived in."

We walked outside, over the rocky terrain, to the cliffs, to see what Jesus saw when Satan offered him the world if Jesus accepted three challenges: turning stone into bread, throwing himself off the cliffs, and to accept the devil's offer for his allegiance.

"All this I will give You if You will bow down and worship me," Satan says.

I just stood in amazement of the beauty. Behind Jesus would have been the Mediterranean Sea, Mount Carmel and the cities of Joppa and Caesarea. To his right, Jerusalem and Bethlehem. Below him, Jericho. Look hard and you can locate the Moab and Gilead Mountains, and the Dead Sea.

I watched as the other tourists made their way around the site. I also saw tour groups from Germany and Italy. And then I sat down to ponder what I have always wondered.

All of this happened right after Jesus was baptized, and before Jesus began his ministry with his followers. He was alone on the top of that mountain with Satan. So how does this story come to pass in the Bible? There is no mention of it in the book of John, "the one whom Jesus loved most." Luke was not around at the time of Jesus.

Matthew and Mark have the story. But how? Only Jesus could have known about it. He had to confide in Matthew and Mark, but not John, or tell somebody else who did the same. Jesus would have been alone up there, along with angels and demons when he responded to Satan.

"Away from Me, Satan! For it is written, 'Worship the Lord your God, and serve Him only.'"

With that, you realize that the mysteries of the Bible may never be uncovered. But the message stares you in the face, without room for debate.

I walked back out to the cliff one last time. I might not be able to figure out the question of how the temptation story came to be, but I do know this: when our Lord and Savior returns in all his glory, his victory party will be at the top of this mountain.

The same mountain I was now standing on. And quivering.

And then it was to head back down the mountain. A much easier journey, if you didn't mind the abuse.

"Hey Bob, break time in 5 minutes!" "Hey Bob, do you need a shuttle to go down the hill?"

Where was the mercy?

I made it down the steps in less than a half hour, without a break, grabbed a shuttle, then hopped on a bus to the bottom where my group was gathering.

"Bob, you made it!" someone hollered.

"Nothing to it," I lied.

The bus pulled out, and I took one more look up the mountain, 400 meters tall. All I could do was shake my head in wonder.

"Again, the devil took him to a very high mountain and showed him all the kingdoms of the world and their splendor. "All this I will give you," he said, "if you will bow down and worship me." Jesus said to him, "Away from me, Satan! For it is written: 'Worship the Lord your God, and serve him only. Then the devil left him, and angels came and attended him."

CHAPTER 15

The Sea of Galilee

"Passing alongside the Sea of Galilee, he saw Simon and Andrew the brother of Simon casting a net into the sea, for they were fishermen. And Jesus said to them, 'Follow me, and I will make you become fishers of men.' And immediately they left their nets and followed him."

"The boat is always empty"

Destination: Holy Land

I knew long before I got off the tour bus that the Sea of Galilee would be a very difficult emotional stopping point for me. Wonderful and incredible for sure, but difficult. This is where Jesus found his disciples and made them fishers of men. This is where he walked on water and calmed the storm. And now, this was where science was calling.

For me, I knew this would be one of many highlights of my journey through the Holy Land.

We made our way down to the Sea, also known as Lake Tiberias, and watched as Anton pointed to a large old wooden boat that was on display by the shore.

"They call this 'The Jesus Boat,'" he told the group. "Two fishermen found this boat on the northwest shore of the sea, sticking from the mud during a drought in 1986. Archeologists have dated the boat to the first century."

Everyone gathered close. This was a must see. The ancient boat was about 30 feet long and less than 10 feet wide. It was completely assembled. And it would have been exactly the same type of boat used by fishermen during the time of Jesus as they fished in the Sea of Galilee.

We were all looking in wonderment at the boat when a woman asked Anton the question we were all thinking.

"The first century?" she asked. "Found on the Sea of Galilee? So are you saying it is possible……."

And she left it there. We all looked at The Walking Encyclopedia, who was beaming.

"Well, we know Jesus was right here in the first century," he said. "And we know this boat was right here in the first century."

Everyone paused and looked around.

"And we know what happened with Jesus and boats on the Sea of Galilee," said Anton's nephew Ayob.

Yes we do. We certainly do.

"Hop on board!" we heard a man holler. I looked out at the sea and saw a boat waiting for our group. We were going for a boat ride, on a modern vessel, onto the Sea of Galilee. As the boat headed out on the peaceful waters, the captain began talking about the sea's history, and I stared out onto the water, closed my eyes, and my mind wandered. I kept listening as the captain filled in the blanks of our journey.

The Sea of Galilee

The sea itself is not that large, measuring less than 15 miles long and under 10 feet wide, he told us. We learned it was also fairly shallow, with a maximum depth around 200 feet in spots.

I opened my eyes, and then I saw it. An empty boat, sitting alone, not moving, anchored on the sea.

A man sitting near me watched me look at it and said "It is to commemorate the boat the disciples were on when Jesus walked to them on the water."

I turned to the man. "The boat is always empty?" I asked.

He smiled and nodded.

"Always anchored?' I asked.

"Empty and anchored," he said.

"It never leaves the sea."

All I could do was stare in amazement. How cool.

And then the boat captain pulled us alongside the empty boat, and told the same story, and asked us this question: "Can you picture Jesus walking on this water, right next to you, right now by the empty boat?"

Yes I can, I thought. I can think about it all day and all night. I knew right then that I would never, ever forget the site of that empty anchored boat.

"......Shortly before dawn Jesus went out to them, walking on the lake. When the disciples saw him walking on the lake, they were terrified. "It's a ghost," they said, and cried out in fear. But Jesus immediately said to them: "Take courage! It is I. Don't be afraid......."

You think about the miracles in the Bible: water into wine; Lazarus raised from the dead; demons cast from bodies. And then you picture the Son of Man calmly walking on the water, raising his arms, and stopping the storm.

Right on the water in front of me.

As our boat returned to shore, I kept staring at the empty, anchored boat. And thought about what that moment must have been like for the disciples to see Jesus calming the storm and walking on the water. To have lived then, to have been there then......

"All ashore!" the boat's captain awakened me from my thoughts. And we all headed back to land. I stepped off the boat realizing in the past 30 minutes I had seen a boat discovered from Jesus' time, a symbolic boat anchored in the water, and floated on the water he walked on. It was a lot to take in.

And I had no idea what was about to come next.

As I walked ashore, I looked to my left, downward to a cove where a group of people had gathered by the waters shore. I wondered what was there.

I glanced at Ayob, who was smiling at me.

"You better get down there, Bob."

I started to make my way down, and watched as people were taking off their sandals and walking into the water. And then it hit me. The shore. The cove. The fishers of men.

Oh my, oh my, oh my.

I looked back at Ayob again who smiled and nodded.

I rushed down the hill, reached the water, threw off my shoes, and rushed in with the others. I raised my arms and looked up at the sky. And then I knelt.

"*....I touch the sky when my knees hit the ground......*"

Time stood still. Tears soon came. I never wanted to leave. I looked back up the hill and saw Gretta Couri from our group heading my way. She was the person most responsible for me being on the trip, and had adopted me and looked after me during our journey. I knew I had to get her down here.

She saw me walking up to meet her. I was soaking wet.

"Bob, did you go in the water?" she asked.

"Gretta, it is more than just water," I told her.

She looked at the cove, all the people, and then back at me.

"Bob?" she said, her eyes getting wide.

"This is it," I told her. "Right here, right now."

She looked again at the cove.

"Go," I told her. "Take your sandals off and go."

I watched as she rushed to the water, a woman I found to be so deep in her faith that I was envious. She reached the water, waded in, and waved back up at me. Another soul visiting with our Lord.

Fishers of Men.

How much more could my emotions, now raw, take in one day? Fortunately, it was time for the bus to head home.

As our bus left the Sea, I could hear everyone else talking about what they had seen: they were experiencing everything that I had experienced; the old boat; the empty boat; the fisherman's cove.

"That old boat was here when he was," a woman said.

"Can you imagine,'" another man said, "that this is where he walked on the water?"

"I can't believe I just walked in the water where he met Peter, and John," a woman said.

"And Andrew, and James," said someone else.

Everyone around me was buzzing with excitement. This was our loudest bus ride yet. I thought back to how solemn and quiet our ride was after visiting Jesus' birth site.

Me? I just closed my eyes and gave thanks to God that I lived long enough to see this day.

Back at home, as the days, weeks and months rolled by, I thought of my many stops in the Holy Land. And at night, as I lay in bed surrounded by darkness, I keep picturing the Sea of Galilee: an old boat, an empty boat, and me, on my knees where fishers became men.

How do you put a price tag on that?

Chills go through my body, and I smile and nod off to sleep.

"And when he got into the boat, his disciples followed him. And behold, there arose a great storm on the sea, so that the boat was being swamped by the waves; but he was asleep. And they went and woke him, saying, "Save us, Lord; we are perishing." And he said to them, "Why are you afraid, O you of little faith?" Then he rose and rebuked the winds and the sea, and there was a great calm. And the men marveled, saying, "What sort of man is this, that even winds and sea obey him?........"

CHAPTER 16

Cana

"On the third day there was a wedding in Cana of Galilee, and the mother of Jesus was there. Jesus and his disciples had also been invited to the wedding. When the wine gave out, the mother of Jesus said to him, "They have no wine." And Jesus said to her, "Woman, what concern is that to you and to me? My hour has not yet come."

"Do whatever he tells you"

CANA

When you think of the Holy Land, you probably think of the manger scene in Bethlehem, or Jesus nailed to the cross in Jerusalem. Those, obviously, are must see sights for any visitor.

But there is one sight that more people visit in the Holy Land each year than any other, and it is not in Bethlehem or Jerusalem. In fact, more people visit it than visit the Vatican in Rome. In a given year, nearly one million of them. And yet despite this, not a single hotel in town.

It's Cana, a Muslim village of about 25,000 people, nestled in the mountains of the lower Galilee. Or maybe it isn't. That's because the exact location of Cana is still being debated by Biblical scholars. Some argue the ancient Cana is actually either Qana or Ain Qana, in Lebanon; others claim it to be either Kafr Kanna, Khirbet Qana or Karm er-Rasm in Israel.

Our visit, the sight where Jesus performed his first miracle, is Kafr Kanna, about three miles outside of Nazareth on the road to Tiberias. The city is now in total ruins, but still with charm. It's a clean village, sitting on a hill, surrounded by trees.

Down the street is the house of Nathaniel. This is where Jesus called Nathaniel, also known as Bartholomew, and his friend Phillip to follow him as disciples.

Most importantly, there is a large spring of water nearby, surrounded by a wall.

Water that was miraculously one day turned into wine.

This is where Jesus performed his first miracle, where a wedding party he was attending ran out of wine. What was the bridal party to do? But clearly, Jesus had no intention of stepping into his world that day, and in fact, was rude when his mother whispered her request into his ear.

"They have no more wine," Mary told him.

Jesus just shook his head.

"Woman, why do you involve me? My time has not yet come."

He was not ready.

But Mary had other ideas, and her actions that day should not be overlooked, because it tells us something very important.

She knew. She had waited a long time. And now she pushed her son.

"Do whatever he tells you," she tells the waiters.

And just as Mary knew, Jesus must have known too. If he provided more wine, it would be the end of his human life as he knew it, and the beginning of his public ministry.

And it would be the beginning of the end of his life, and his journey to the cross.

A sign leading into the village of Kafr Kanna proclaims the wedding miracle. There are three churches here, the Church of St. George, the Chapel of Bartholomew, and the Church of the Marriage Feast, or what has become known as "The Wedding Church."

The latter is where people were cramming.

At the Church of the Marriage Feast the wine miracle is transcribed on the wall as you walk in. You see memorials from the 4th century. The floor has glass tiles you can look under and see ancient inscriptions. The church has two columns, and very small pews. Upon the altar are six jars. A huge jar, carved in stone, sits nearby.

And then you see two large stone jars.

"These are believed to be two of the original water pots," Anton tells our group.

And we stare.

So why do more people come to Cana than anywhere else in the Holy Land?

"We are going to renew our wedding vows," said a couple from Cleveland sitting next to me. "What better place to do it than at the most famous wedding site of all time?"

And they were not alone. Inside the church, people had lined up to be married again. Some walked in wearing their shorts and sandals, others in tuxedos and dresses they brought across the oceans. So many couples that the only option was a one mass, quick ceremony for everyone.

"Dearly beloved, we are gathered here today......"

"Do you take this man?"

"I do!"

"Do you take this woman?"

"I do!"

"I now pronounce you man and wife. You may kiss the bride."

Tiny packets of rice sit nearby, waiting to be thrown.

We departed the church to find the streets of Kafr Kanna filled with vendors selling souvenir bottles of "Cana wedding wine." Everybody got in line. I wondered how much of the wine would really make it back home.

I walked into a group where another tour guide was speaking. She was telling her tourists about the different cities all claiming to be the site of the original Cana, and why she was skeptical of Kafr Kanna.

CANA

"About five miles north of here is Khirbet Qana," she said. "They have found a tunnel there with crosses, and phrases referring to 'Lord Jesus. I tend to lean that way."

Of course, I had to sneak in a quick question.

"With numerous villages claiming to be the original Cana, why do most tour buses come here?" I asked.

"Look around," she said. "A church calling itself "The Wedding Church" offering mass weddings. Vendors everywhere. They have done a good job here to attract visitors. But Kafr Kanna was not even considered a possible Cana sight until a couple of hundred years ago."

Like many of the tourist sites, nobody knows exactly where something is, or occurred. It mattered little to me or the other tourists. We came to relive the moment, to picture it in our minds forever.

I left the group and walked a few blocks to Cana Bells restaurant, just to pop in, look at the menu, and see if I risked snagging anything.

I did not.

Down the street was May and Nabhan's gift shop. A sign above the small store says "Fill the Jars with Water." Inside, the store knew what sold, and that was wine. You could find a bottle of their special dry red wine, aged for a year, for around $50. Bargain hunters, unconcerned about the quality of wine, could find something around $15.

I bumped into the happy couple from Cleveland who had renewed their wedding vows.

"Well, how was it?" I asked.

"A little larger than our first wedding," the man smiled.

"And a little louder," his wife said. "Everybody is screaming 'I do' at the same time."

I reached into my pocket where I still had a little pocket of the church rice.

"May I?" I asked.

"Please do," the blushing bride said.

And with that they bowed their heads and I dunked them with some more rice. Not just any rice, but rice from Cana, or whatever town we were in that wanted to be Cana.

"You should have brought your wife with you," her husband said. "You guys could have been married again."

I smiled.

"You are assuming she would have said 'I do'," I laughed.

With that, we headed back to our bus, where everyone seemed to have a bottle of wine except me. And sure enough, samples were being passed around.

As we drove, the story of Cana and the water being turned to wine sent my mind wondering backwards. We know very little about Jesus' life growing up. But surely, he must have known. Mary knew. Joseph had to know. What about Jesus' siblings and cousins? Did they know? Was it a secret? If Jesus was 30 years old at Cana, and that was his first miracle, what was his life like before that?

And then you hear Mary speak those five words that we can all live by: "Do whatever he tells you."

He told us at the Sermon on the Mount. He told us at the Last Supper. He told us on the cross. He told us on his resurrection.

"And surely I am with you always, to the very end of the age."

The bus rolled through the mountainside. I kept thinking about Jesus, the wine miracle, and wondered again how Jesus and his followers walked the land.

"Next stop, St. Anne's," the bus driver announced.

Another church, I thought. I could not have been more wrong.

"Nearby stood six stone water jars, the kind used by the Jews for ceremonial washing, each holding from twenty to thirty gallons. Jesus said to the servants, "Fill the jars with water"; so they filled them to the brim. Then he told them, "Now draw some out and take it to the master of the banquet. What Jesus did here in Cana of Galilee was the first of the signs through which he revealed his glory; and his disciples believed in him."

CHAPTER 17

The Church of St. Anne

"Some time later, Jesus went up to Jerusalem for one of the Jewish festivals. Now there is in Jerusalem near the Sheep Gate a pool, which in Aramaic is called Bethesda and which is surrounded by five covered colonnades. Here a great number of disabled people used to lie—the blind, the lame, the paralyzed. One who was there had been an invalid for thirty-eight years. When Jesus saw him lying there and learned that he had been in this condition for a long time, he asked him, "Do you want to get well?" "Sir," the invalid replied, "I have no one to help me into the pool when the water is stirred. While I am trying to get in, someone else goes down ahead of me. Then Jesus said to him, "Get up! Pick up your mat and walk." At once the man was cured; he picked up his mat and walked."

Our first stop this day was The Church of St. Anne, located just north of Jerusalem's Damascus Gate. The original church was built around 450 AD, and the current church dates to around 1140 AD. It is the most preserved church in Jerusalem, sitting next to the Pools of Bethesda, where Jesus performed many of his healings.

Destination: Holy Land

"Spirit lead me where my trust is without borders"

There were two pools that were used by Jerusalem residents as rainwater preserves. People who had disabilities would lay by the Bethesda pool, believing its waters had magical powers to heal them. Legend has it that an angel would fly over the pools one time every day, and whoever happened to be inside the water at that exact moment in time would be miraculously healed.

The church is located in the Muslim Quarter, with bustling streets outside. It is surrounded by a large courtyard with trees and flowers.

Before I entered the church, I strolled past The Message Cafe, a small quaint coffee shop. A worker inside was asking the tourists if they came to sing. It seemed like a strange question and most of us moved on.

The Church of St. Anne

On this day, it was September, and it was very hot in Jerusalem.

"No matter how hot it is outside," a woman entering the church next to me said, "it is always nice and cool inside."

I was all for that.

"And don't forget to sing," she said. "This is the best place to sing in the world."

I looked at her puzzled, and remembered what the man at the coffee shop had said.

"Surrounded by others," I told her, "I can stand and quietly sing with the best of them."

She just smiled.

"What?" I asked.

"Wait and see," she said. "Wait and see."

Just inside the church is a statue of Anne with her daughter Miriam (Mary). As you enter, you are struck by the church's simplicity. There is little consistency in the design. There is no fancy interior or floor, just giant pillars. Even the size of the windows are different.

The church site is believed to be the home of Mary's parents, and Jesus' grandparents, Anne and Joachim. This would be the birthplace of the Virgin Mary, and the church was named after her mother. At the altar of the church are three episodes of Mary's life; on the right is the Annunciation; on the left is the nativity of Jesus; and in the middle is the descent of Jesus from the cross.

You take the stone steps down from the altar and head to the crypt. It is a cave that has the remains of Mary's childhood home.

As I headed back up the steps, I began hearing the noise, the singing from a distance. With each step, it became louder and more beautiful.

> "…..Oh Lord, my God,
> When I, in awesome wonder
> Consider all the worlds Thy hands have made
> I see the stars, I hear the rolling thunder
> Thy power throughout the universe displayed….."

I began trying to walk faster, to hear more clearly. I reach the top, and I see them.

> "….Then sings my soul, my Saviour God, to thee:
> How great thou art! How great thou art!
> Then sings my soul, my Saviour God, to thee:
> How great thou art! How great thou art!...."

Destination: Holy Land

A pilgrimage group was singing on stage. It was beyond beautiful. The acoustics in the church were amazing. I stood in awe and watched the group exit the stage, and then saw a woman, alone, slowly walk up to the front. She was going to sing.

> "......Holy, holy, holy!
> Lord God Almighty! /
> Early in the morning our song shall rise to thee...."

I soon realize that what I am watching is beyond anything I have ever seen. Random people, from around the world, walking up on stage without fear and singing in front of strangers, one after another."

> "...Holy, holy, holy!
> Merciful and mighty /
> God in three persons, blessed Trinity!..."

Stunned at how beautiful this was, I watch her leave the stage, to be followed by an African group of men.

> "......Amazing grace how sweet the sound
> That saved a wretch like me
> I once was lost but now I'm found
> Was blind but now I see......"

This is amazing, one of the most incredible things I have ever seen. I never want to leave. It was as if the angels were singing.

> "..... Twas grace that taught my heart to fear,
> and grace my fears relieved;
> how precious did that grace appear
> The hour I first believed......"

I look behind me to my right, and I see the woman I walked in with. She smiles, then points to me and then points to the stage.

No, no way, I shake my head. I mean, I really want to, I would love to, but surely I cannot.

I sit and I think. Could I do it? What would I sing? Others are coming on the stage now. My mind is racing. Okay, I've got it. I know the words. I sing them to myself, quietly, every day.

> "....... You call me out upon the waters
> The great unknown where feet may fail
> And there I find You in the mystery
> In oceans deep my faith will stand......"

The Church of St. Anne

I am ready to sing. I stand up and get in line. And then my tour group announces they are leaving. I look back and they are heading out the door. The woman I walked in with is smiling and shaking her head.

I catch up with my group wondering if it might have been worth it to be left behind, just so I could have the chance to sing. Surely they would have missed me, and come back for me. That thought did not last long, and I raced for the bus. And on my way, as I passed people looking at me strangely, I saw no reason to contain myself.

> *"…..Spirit lead me where my trust is without borders*
> *Let me walk upon the waters*
> *Wherever You would call me*
> *Take me deeper than my feet could ever wander*
> *And my faith will be made stronger*
> *In the presence of my Saviour……."*

Wow. Did I feel fulfilled. I caught up with the bus, hopped on and listened to people talk about their day. Some mentioned the Bethsaida pools, others talked about going into the Muslim quarter. And then a man mentioned St. Anne's church and looked my way.

"Bob, didn't I see you inside the church?" he asked.

"Yes, you did," I said. "It was wonderful."

"You were in line, getting ready to sing," he said.

Everyone began looking at me.

"Um, not really….." I began.

"No you were, I saw you get up and get in the line."

And then he smiled. "Maybe you would like to sing for us now?"

Like the cat swallowing the canary, I just shook my head.

"We could pass the hat," he laughed. "Take up a collection?"

"Not happening," I said. "The next time I sing, it will be in the shower."

It is my biggest regret from the trip. If you go to St. Anne's, sing. Walk up to that altar, look to the heavens, and sing loud and proud like it's the last words you will ever speak.

"The day on which this took place was a Sabbath, and so the Jewish leaders said to the man who had been healed, "It is the Sabbath; the law forbids you to carry your mat. But he replied, "The man who made me well said to me, 'Pick up your mat and walk.' So they asked him, "Who is this fellow who told you to pick it up and walk?" The man

who was healed had no idea who it was, for Jesus had slipped away into the crowd that was there. Later Jesus found him at the temple and said to him, "See, you are well again. Stop sinning or something worse may happen to you". The man went away and told the Jewish leaders that it was Jesus who had made him well."

CHAPTER 18

The Mount of Beatitudes

"He went down with them and stood on a level place. A large crowd of his disciples was there and a great number of people from all over Judea, from Jerusalem, and from the coastal region around Tyre and Sidon, who had come to hear him and to be healed of their diseases. Those troubled by impure spirits were cured, and the people all tried to touch him, because power was coming from him and healing them all."

"Beati pauperes spiritu"

You stand on top of the mountain and look around. It is impossible not to take everything in.

The book of Genesis, and the relationship between God and his creations. The book of Exodus, and how God is to be worshiped. The book of Leviticus, and the regulations for his people. The book of Deuteronomy, and God's reminder to all of us.

Of all places on my trip, this may have been the one where I could stand, close my eyes, and see it perfectly in my mind; Jesus standing. Jesus speaking. Jesus teaching.

The Beatitudes are sitting on a hill that oversees the Sea of Galilee. Further out are the Golan Heights. With mountains and hilltops everywhere, the exact site of Jesus' Sermon on the Mount is often debated. But this is close to the highest point you can see. You look down and can see Capernaum, just a few miles away, where Jesus did most of his teachings. There could be no better place for him to speak to the masses than here.

There is a modest, octagon shaped church on site for visitors, built in 1938 called the Church of the Beatitudes. An ancient church dating back to the fourth century would have been nearby. In front of it is a beautiful garden with places for worship. There is a guest house close by, and you watch as outdoor services are being held, with visitors from all over the world.

You look up at the ceiling as you enter the temple and see windows with each of the sermon verses, written in Latin. "Beati pauperes spiritu......"

Blessed are the poor in spirit.

There is a large open gallery inside. In the center is the altar of the temple, where a cross hangs, with scenes of both the crucifixion and ascension next to it. As you walk up to it you notice on the floor are the seven symbols of human virtues that Jesus often preached: Justice, Kindness, Discretion, Faith, Valor, Hope and Modesty. You look out the windows and can see the Sea of Galilee in the distance.

Below the temple is a place called Sower's Cove, where Jesus taught the Parable of the Sower from a boat. I love how that one ends: "Whoever has ears to hear, let them hear!"

I walked around the chapel and looked at all the pilgrims praying. I spotted a small group of Franciscan Sisters watching from the side, and approached them. I told them I was writing a book about my journey.

"Hello Bob. My name is Sister Telesphora," she said. "This is Sister Marcelle. Tell us about your journey."

"Well, we just left St. Anne's Church," I smiled.

The Mount of Beatitudes

"And did you sing?" Sister Marcelle asked.

They both laughed as I sadly shook my head.

I asked about the church, the mountain, and living so close to God and Jesus.

"When the day ends, and it is quiet here, it is so peaceful," Sister Telesphora said. "We feel presence all the time, but especially at that time."

I thanked them, and walked back outside. They were right. Peaceful was the word. There is contentment here, knowing you are following the will of God.

This was the Sermon on the Mount. And of course, the Mount of Beatitudes is also where Jesus met his disciples after the Resurrection. Two incredible moments in history on the same spot.

We had a few minutes to linger, and I walked back outside and looked for a rock to sit on and pray. Then I pulled out the notecard I had written on before getting on the bus that morning. And then I began reading quietly, but out loud, to myself.

> Blessed are the poor in spirit, for theirs is the Kingdom of Heaven.
> Blessed are those who weep, for they will be comforted.
> Blessed are the meek, for they will inherit the earth.
> Blessed are those who hunger and thirst for righteousness,
>   for they will be satisfied.
> Blessed are the merciful, for they will have mercy.
> Blessed are the pure in heart, for they will see God.
> Blessed are the peacemakers, for they will be called sons of God.
> Blessed are those banished for righteousness, for theirs is the
>   Kingdom of Heaven.

Jesus is talking to the masses about being happy. But He does not use the word happy. He uses the word Blessed. Blessed will lead to happiness. He is giving us the road map. When you read the Sermon on the Mount, Jesus is not lecturing the crowd. He is not moralizing. This is not God giving Moses the Ten Commandments. Jesus is speaking as the Son of God, speaking to the least among us. He is teaching us what it means to be a good, decent, compassionate human being. Jesus is preaching about a revolution. Each of us is somewhere among those blessed. And that happiness we are seeking? It is knowing you are being blessed by God. If you are a follower of Jesus, then you need to live the words.

I put the card back in my pocket and noticed a woman standing behind me. She was smiling.

Destination: Holy Land

"That was wonderful," she said.

I nodded and whispered, "thank you."

"It is hard to put into words," she said. "I just feel his presence here. If only we knew where the exact spot was……."

Her voice trailed off, and I watched her look at all the mountain tops around her.

"That would be incredible," I told her. "But this is the most likely area."

Just as we finished speaking, Anton, the encyclopedia himself, looked our way and called the group over.

"There is one more thing you might be interested in seeing before we go," he tells us.

I watch as he points to an area that is above the temple.

"This area is called Mughara Ayub," he says. "Most historians believe his is believed to be the spot where Jesus stood and gave his Sermon on the Mount."

And then I watched as a group of 50 of us just stood and stared, mouths open in silence. I looked at the woman who I was talking with minutes ago. She was clutching her rosary. She looked at me and smiled. I waved her over to me, and handed her my card.

"Let's sit," I told her. "It is your turn."

She took my card and began reading out loud.

> Blessed are the poor in spirit, for theirs is the Kingdom of Heaven.
> Blessed are those who weep, for they will be comforted.
> Blessed are the meek, for they will inherit the earth.
> Blessed are those who hunger and thirst for righteousness,
>   for they will be satisfied.

And then I joined her.

> Blessed are the merciful, for they will have mercy.
> Blessed are the pure in heart, for they will see God.
> Blessed are the peacemakers, for they will be called sons of God.
> Blessed are those banished for righteousness, for theirs is the
>   Kingdom of Heaven.

We finished and I told her I was writing a book about my travels. I asked her if I could use her name.

"I'm Debbie," she said. "I'm from Philly. This is my bucket list."

"A bucket list? Really?" I asked. "You, me and a thousand of our friends," I said as I pointed at the crowd.

The Mount of Beatitudes

We stood up and looked out over the mountain. It was as if nobody could walk away. Finally, another group behind us was entering, and we began to leave. As we passed them, I saw their shirts say they were from Hong Kong. A man in the back of their group looked my way. I smiled and nodded at him. He put his hands in prayer, bowed his head, then looked back up at me. I then did the same to him. We repeated this a couple of times. I walked over and stuck out my hand.

"Bob, from America."

"I am Pak, from Hong Kong."

Two complete strangers from opposite ends of the planet sharing their faith. Priceless.

I took one last look down the mountain top before leaving, and I kept thinking of the same question: what could possibly have changed from this view over the past 2,000 years? And the answer was clear. Nothing.

Just an amazing experience. Never to be forgotten. Ever.

"And when Jesus finished these sayings, the crowds were astonished at his teaching, for he was teaching them as one who had authority, and not as their scribes."

CHAPTER 19

Magdala

"Soon afterward he went on through cities and villages, proclaiming and bringing the good news of the Kingdom of God. And the twelve were with him, and also some women who had been healed of evil spirits and infirmities: Mary, called Magdalene, from whom seven demons had gone out."

"The Magdala Stone"

I think back to all of my heroes in the Bible. I think of Noah and Abraham, of Moses and David, of Peter and John, of Paul and Luke.

And then I think of Mary Magdalene.

She was likely the first woman who accompanied Jesus on his journey. He drove seven demons from her body. She was with Christ at the cross, standing next to his mother, when the rest of his disciples had abandoned him. And of course, It is Mary who Jesus appears to first at his resurrection.

Any list of biblical heroes must have Mary Magdalene's name near the top.

When I saw our itinerary for the day was a visit to the tiny town of Magdala, Mary's town, I looked forward to the usual, a church, possibly the sight of where a house she grew up in once sat among the ruins. Some display in town honoring her.

I was in for a gigantic, wonderful surprise.

We pulled into what was now a very small village on the shore of the Galilee, not even listed on some maps anymore.

"What you see today is not what Jesus would have seen 2,000 years ago," our guide Ayob told the group. "Magdala was a big city back during the time of Jesus, one of the largest in the Galilee area, with hundreds of fishing boats that would have been in the water every day."

And then the bus stopped, and Ayob's grandfather Anton stood up.

"You will see something today that you will not forget for the rest of your life," he said.

I looked to my right and saw Aggie Couri. Her eyes were wide as she looked at me.

"Let's go Bob!" she said. "We can't miss this."

We hurried off the bus, and gathered near a small pavilion. I looked out among a gated field of rocks and ruins.

What could it possibly be?

Anton led us to the center of the field.

"What you are looking at is the Migdal Synagogue. It is the oldest synagogue found in Galilee."

As we looked out among all of the ruins, there, sitting right in the middle, was a large, nearly pristine piece. Anton led us right to it.

"And there, my friends," he paused, "is what is known as the Magdala Stone."

The stone was pure, while everything around it was not. There were carvings on the top, and all four sides of the stone, representing a menorah, and clearly symbols meant to depict the temple in Jerusalem. Incredibly, it had survived the rigors of time and weather and destruction.

Quite simply, it had to be among the most incredible archaeological pieces ever discovered.

"How old?" a man from our group shouted from behind me.

"I get that question all the time," Anton smiled. "We can date this stone to just after the time of Jesus' death."

There was a murmur among the group.

"That makes this stone the earliest known image ever found in a synagogue," Anton said. "The symbols on the stone are similar to the symbols in the first chapter of the book of Ezekiel."

Now the murmur went to silence. I looked over at Aggie. I wondered if my eyes were as big as hers.

"And it means that this synagogue," Anton hollered to the group, "was likely here during the time of Jesus, and he likely stood right here, right where you are standing, right now preaching in this very spot."

I looked over at Aggie again and nodded.

No one in the group said a word. We just stared at Anton and the stone.

"The stone would have held the Torah scrolls that were read on Shabbat," Anton said. "Jesus would have stood in front of it, reading and preaching. Everyone, take a minute."

A minute? I could have stood there a lifetime. His presence was with me now, more than ever.

You get on an airplane, fly halfway around the world, and you wonder if your dreams will ever come true. And then they keep coming true, day after day after day. How many times can chills go through your body? How many tears can you possibly spill?

For me and my faith, the answers are never enough. Keep the chills and tears coming.

We started walking in a circle around the Magdala stone.

"They began excavating this site about 15 years ago," Anton shouted to the group. "But it wasn't just the stone they found. There was more."

What? There was more in this tiny village of ruins?

"They found four beautiful Jewish purification baths, nearly intact," Anton said. "They found a coin dating to the time when Jesus was alive."

More murmurs in the crowd.

"So the archeologists kept digging, and what else did they find?" Anton asked.

Now I could only stare at the Walking Encyclopedia, and wait for what came next.

"The ancient village of Magdala was only about a foot underground!"

That was hard to believe. And so is what came next.

"They aren't finished. Only about ten percent of the ancient town has been uncovered so far."

I looked at a man standing next to me.

"Can you go get us a couple of shovels," he laughed. "I will stay and dig."

"Right with you," I told him.

"Come," Anton told the group. "We have more to see."

The group moved into a chapel overlooking the Sea of Galilee, where the altar was made out of a boat, similar to the fishing boats that would have been in the sea at the time Jesus was there. As you walk closer, the altar is beautifully lined up against open glass, looking as if it is sitting on the sea.

As the group prepared for mass, I made my way back towards the ruins, where I could see workers digging in the distance. I bumped into Father Eamon Kelly from Magdala.

"You know," I told him, "today would be a good time to find something. I am standing right here!"

He laughed.

"Well, they have already found a lot. We have some coins that date back to when Jesus would have been about five years old. We have one of them from 29 AD, the exact time Jesus would have been teaching in this synagogue. We found a room where the torah scrolls would have been stored. It is just amazing."

As my eyes widened, Father Kelly made me an offer.

"Come, I am going on my daily stroll. I walk for miles and miles every day."

"I would love to Father," I began, thinking desperately of a way out of more exercise. "But my group, I am not sure how long before they are leaving."

He smiled.

"I am just going up and down the shoreline of the Galilee. I do it every morning at sunrise. Are you sure?"

"I really wish I had more time, but I also want to sample a quick snack......." I began.

We shook hands and said goodbye. I promised him I would be following the excavation story of Magdala.

I walked across the street to the Cafe Vero. Today's special was the Saint Peter fish. I watched them bring a plate out. It was an entire fish, head, eyes, and all.

Like the exercise, I decided to pass on the snack and headed back to my group. I passed a brand new hotel on site, a recognition that ancient discoveries from a town now longer on the map will bring in visitors from around the world. For $300 a night you can enjoy an outdoor pool and gym, a fine dining restaurant, then walk out the front door and turn back the hands of time two thousand years.

Try doing that back home.

I found my group back at the chapel. They asked where I had been.

"Just took my walk. Getting my daily exercise, you know. Oh, and I grabbed a snack."

Everyone knew my habits by now. Nobody was buying.

We left the chapel and walked out. And I realized that the excavations will continue. And someday, somewhere very near where I was standing, they would find Mary Magdalene's home. She was the Apostle to the Apostles.

"I have seen the Lord!" she was the first to tell them.

She is at the top of my hero list.

As we got back to the bus, I again looked at Aggie.

"How cool was that?" I asked her.

I did not need to wait for an answer. Her eyes told the story.

"Those who ate were four thousand men, besides women and children. And after sending away the crowds, he got into the boat and went to the region of Magadala."

CHAPTER 20

Mount Tabor

"And after six days Jesus took with him Peter and James, and John, his brother, and led them up a high mountain by themselves. And he was transfigured before them, and his face shone like the sun, and his clothes became white as light. And behold, there appeared to them Moses and Elijah, talking with him."

Unlike our visit to Magdala, which gave me a wonderful surprise, I knew exactly what was coming at Mount Tabor. There would be many incredible holy sites on my journey, but this one would need no introduction.

Mount Tabor dates all the way back to the Book of Judges, more than 1,000 years before the birth of Jesus. It was here where Deborah told Barak to gather his troops and prepare for war against the Canaanites. For me and the rest of our group, this was the site of the transfiguration. This was Jesus, Moses, and Elijah on a mountaintop, staring at the face of God.

And Unlike Jesus, Peter, and the Sons of Thunder, I had an air conditioned bus ride to take me to the top of the mountain. Our bus driver was kind enough to ask if anyone preferred to walk.

After our previous mountain experiences, no one took him up on the offer. Once again, the bus could only make it so far up the hill, before it had to stop and we were transferred to waiting cars. The mountain was too steep, the roads to windy. The cars could only move at a camel's pace.

It is impossible to miss Mount Tabor. It towers over the region, by far the tallest mountain in the area around Galilee, reaching more than six football fields into the sky. You look to the east and you can see the Gilboa

Mountains. To the west are the Carmel Mountains, and to the north are the Golan Heights. Ruins are sprinkled along the hilltop.

There is roughly a two mile trail at the top of the mountain that circles the Church of the Transfiguration, built around 100 years ago. There are two towers at the entrance for visitors, leading to chapels for Moses and Elijah. Inside is a large golden mosaic that tells the story of the Transfiguration. The walls are inscribed with the words of Matthew describing the events to the world. There are paintings that depict scenes from both the old and new testaments. Walking down the steps of the church you will find a stone that legend says comes from the transfiguration.

"His face shone like the sun, and his clothes became as white as the light. Just then there appeared before them Moses and Elijah, talking with Jesus."

And there is where I pause. And a question that I had longed to have answered. Like the Garden of Gethsemane, the transfiguration is a biblical story told from a distance. Jesus brought John, Peter and James with him. But the story is told only through the writings of Matthew. And Matthew was standing down below, at the foot of the mountain, those six football fields below, with the other disciples. Like Matthew, John wrote a gospel. John, the disciple 'Jesus loved most.' But John makes no mention of the event. Why would he not write about such an incredible moment? Matthew's account, as wonderful as it is, is one of the rare stories in the gospel's that is not eye witnessed.

"A bright cloud covered them, and a voice from the cloud said, "This is my Son, whom I love; with him I am well pleased. Listen to him!"

John witnesses Jesus with Moses and Elijah, hears the voice of God, and does not write it? I needed an explanation. There was only one way to find out. The Encyclopedia.

"You know," I told Anton, "John was here with Jesus, Moses and Elijah, but he never wrote about it. I found that odd."

Anton, by now on the trip amused by questions, smiled.

"Look at the timing of the gospels Bob," Anton told me. "John's gospel was likely the last one written. He knew Matthew and Mark were already writing about Jesus, and Matthew's was written much, much earlier. John may not have wanted to repeat what Matthew had already written."

"Yes," I said. "But this is Moses, this is Elijah, this is the face of God......"

Anton smiled again, enjoying his opportunity for the teacher to teach the student. "Jesus told many parables that are spread throughout the gospel, did he not?"

"Of course he did," I said.

"Do you know how many of those parable's are told in the Gospel of John?" he asked.

I shook my head no. I did not. Where could he be going with this?

"He did not write about any of them," Anton said, smiling again. "John knew that those parables were already written elsewhere by Matthew and Mark. Perhaps he felt that there was no need for him to repeat them."

And suddenly I had my answer to a question that had always intrigued me. The man is indeed a walking encyclopedia. If I could only take him home with me to answer every other question I had in life.

"Are we good, Bob?" he asked.

"As always," I said. "Thank you."

I walk away, smarter than two minutes earlier, and make my way down ancient stairs to the lower chapel of the church where you could see ruins, the same ruins that are spread throughout the mountain. A sign nearby tells you that there are 400 different plant species that have been recorded in the area.

I then headed outside the church and came across a statue of Pope Paul the 6th, with a caption declaring he was the first pope in more than a thousand years to visit the Holy Land.

What? It took a pope 1,000 years to visit the Holy Land?

I slowly made my way back over to The Encyclopedia, who saw me coming out of the corner of his eye. I pointed to the statue.

"That statue about Pope Paul visiting the mountain," I began, "the first Pope in a thousand years? How is that possible?"

Anton smiled again.

"Since the beginning of the Catholic Church, there have been 266 Pope's," he said. "Do you know how many of them have ever visited the Holy Land?"

I shook my head. As a non-Catholic, I assumed many, if not most. Why would they not?

"Four," Anton, who is Catholic, said. "Four out of Two hundred and sixty six."

For the second time on today's journey, I looked how I probably always look, confused.

"You must realize," Anton said, "that Pope Paul was the first Pope to even leave Italy in some 150 years. They never traveled. He was the first Pope to ever even get on an airplane. Let's just say they were a little behind the times."

"But they have traveled all over the world since," I argued. "Surely they might want to see where Jesus was born, or was crucified. Or stand right here where we are now?"

Anton smiled again.

"I am sure they did. But you must also realize, Bob, that the Pope's were not always welcome in the Holy Land. And now, although relations are somewhat better between the religions, the Christian footprint in the Holy Land has dwindled, and is not what it used to be. There is always going to be the question of security, and safety."

I nodded.

"Go enjoy the church," Anton said. "Enjoy the mountain. Come back in five minutes with your next question."

And we laughed.

We began our walk back to our cars, and onto the day's next journey. Ayob walked up next to me.

"Did you learn anything today from my grandfather?" he asked.

"Anything? I learned everything," I said. "Your grandfather is priceless. He should be teaching a Master class somewhere."

"Before this, he taught in high schools for 40 years," Ayob said.

"How do you keep up with….." I started.

"I can't," Ayob laughed. "Nobody can."

We reached the cars, and I looked back one last time at Mount Tabor as Anton gathered the group.

"As you take your cars down the mountain, and then transfer to your buses, think about the disciples walking up and down this mountain. Would someone like to guess how many steps it takes to walk from the bottom to the top?"

Anton looked at me, and I quickly ducked my head toward the ground.

"It takes almost five thousand steps," he said before smiling. "Some of you could use the exercise."

Of course, he had to look at me again.

Mount Tabor

"A bright cloud overshadowed them, and a voice from the cloud said, "This is my beloved Son, with whom I am well pleased; listen to him." When the disciples heard this, they fell on their faces and were terrified. But Jesus came and touched them, saying, "Rise, and have no fear." And when they lifted up their eyes, they saw no one but Jesus only."

CHAPTER 21

Capernaum

"He went down to Capernaum, a city in Galilee, and was teaching them on the Sabbath. They were astounded at his teaching because he spoke with authority. In the synagogue there was a man who had the spirit of an unclean demon, and he cried out with a loud voice, "Leave us alone! What have you to do with us, Jesus of Nazareth? Have you come to destroy us? I know who you are, the Holy One of God." But Jesus rebuked him, saying, "Be quiet and come out of him!" Then the demon, throwing the man down before them, came out of him without doing him any harm. They were all astounded and kept saying to one another, "What kind of word is this, that with authority and power he commands the unclean spirits and they come out?"

"The town of Jesus"

Capernaum

The first thing you see when you pull into the sleepy town is the sign. "Capernaum, the town of Jesus."

But it is not really Capernaum, not anymore. Today the town that sits where Capernaum once sat is called Kfar Nahum. Archaeologists say the town of Capernaum dated back to the 2nd century BC. And today, Kfar Nahum is in total ruins.

You read the Bible and realize that, incredibly, Jesus decided to leave Nazareth. Did he attempt to begin his ministry in his hometown, but did not have success? Something made him pack a bag, and head some 50 miles north, to the Sea of Galilee, eventually landing in Capernaum. Matthew was collecting taxes for Rome from here. Peter, Andrew, John and James were right down the shore on the Sea of Galilee, fishing in their hometown of Bethsaida, just to the north.

Jesus' ministry would have lasted in Capernaum for about three years. He would spend roughly two thirds of his time right in this area. But make no mistake: Capernaum became the epicenter of Jesus' ministry. This is where miracles happened and disciples were taught. It sits on the northern shore of the Sea of Galilee, and you know that everything went down right here in this holy place.

It does not take long to realize how important Jesus quickly became in Capernaum. In the first chapter of Mark, just a couple of minutes after the sun sets one day, Mark writes, "The whole town was gathered at the door." And before the sun rises in the morning, when Jesus goes off to pray, the disciples find him and tell him "Everyone is looking for you."

Today Kfar Nahum looks like a city of ruins, untouched from centuries ago. They say the ruins here date to before Abraham. You look around for people. There are none. Only about 500 people live in Kfar Nahum today, about a third of the size of Jesus' time.

But there was a time.......

Very few places in the Holy Land have been excavated as much as Capernaum. Roman bath houses dating back to the second century have been discovered. Coins have been found from the fourth century.

I followed the group as we walked first to an old synagogue made of white limestone, likely from that same fourth century. But underneath it are remains clearly from a much earlier date. You see a Star of David carved into rocks along the way. There are inscriptions on stones everywhere, written in various languages And there, hanging above the ruins is a modern hexagonal church, near the site where the original synagogue stood two thousand years ago. You walk over a glass floor where you can look down and see the ruins.

Anton brought the group together.

"This church sits on the site of what would have been Peter's home," he said.

I could see everyone looking around and whispering to each other. We had all seen and loved "The Chosen." We could all picture the room. I half expected Eden to walk around the corner with some refreshments. This is where Jesus healed Peter's mother in law; where the paralytic was lowered through the roof.

"When the early excavators began working here," Anton said, "they found walls from the first century. The walls were made of heavy plaster. Archeologists found old oil lamps here," Anton said. "And they found something else, something much more important than a lamp."

As always, the Walking Encyclopedia paused for the full effect of the hammer that he was about to drop on the crowd.

"And on these very walls were many references to Peter."

Again, everyone looked around, realizing where they were standing. And then my eyes saw them: references to Jesus everywhere. They call him Christ. They call him the Lord. They call him the Most High.

And then a reference to God.

"The first building that was built over Peter's house was around 50 AD," Anton said. "There have been several churches built on this site since then. All were destroyed, and Capernaum was left for ruins. But over time, Christians made continuous pilgrimages to this house. They must have had a good reason. It is likely that after Jesus' death, this is where his disciples would have gathered."

Yet you realize that while the people of Capernaum saw Jesus perform more miracles than anywhere else, many there still rejected his preachings, leaving Jesus to ultimately declare "And you, Capernaum, will be thrown down to Hades! I tell you that it will be more tolerable for Sodom on the day of judgment than for you."

We walked outside, and as I usually do, I looked for a place to sit and take notes, and found a stone bench near the old synagogue. I found a woman I recognized from the tour group.

"Hi, I'm Bob," I said. "Do you mind if I sit?"

"Please," she nodded. "I'm Claire."

We looked out at the old synagogue in front of us, and its ancient white stones.

"You are the one writing the book, right?" Claire asked.

"I am," I said. "My bucket list."

"Me too," she said. "I think it is everyone's."

"What is amazing to me," I said, "is that there are stories everywhere. I knew there would be. But then once you sit here……."

"I know," she said. "Anton's grandson Ayob told me to come sit on this stone bench."

I looked at her puzzled. She smiled.

"This is where Jesus would have sat when he taught in the synagogue."

I looked quickly from her to where Ayob was standing. He smiled and nodded.

It took me a few seconds. Claire and I looked around.

"He walked here," she said. "Right on these stones. He taught here, right in that synagogue. I mean, there are stories everywhere, but he did everything right here."

"I know," I said. "We go from place to place, but this was his town. And don't forget, this is where he gathered his followers one last time."

"Will this one be in your book?" she asked.

"You know it will," I said.

"And will you tell them you had tears in your eyes?"

We both laughed. "By now," I said, "I think they would have expected nothing less."

We sat for a few more minutes before Anton called us back to the bus. Another long walk.

"Look around you as you leave," he said. "Remember everything that happened here."

I looked back at the ancient synagogue, then over to Peter's house. I pictured the crippled man being lowered through the roof to be healed. As I began walking I looked out over the Sea of Galilee. I saw fishers of men. I looked out into the water, closed my eyes, and there was Jesus, in the storm, walking on water, pleading with Peter to have faith.

Finally, I was back at the bus.

"Bob?"

I looked up. It was Ayob.

"We are waiting on you," he smiled. "Let's go!"

"Do we have to?" I asked.

"Well, there is a trail down there called the 'Gospel Trail.'" he said. "You can hang around and go for a nice walk if you would like. The trail follows the footsteps of Jesus from Nazareth to Capernaum. I suppose you could walk back and meet us there."

I was actually intrigued. A nice walk back, the same walk Jesus made. How wonderful would that feel.

"How long is the walk?" I asked.

"About 40 miles," Ayob said.

And we laughed.

"I think I will get on the bus now."

"They entered into a ship, and went over the sea toward Capernaum. And it was now dark, and Jesus was not come to them. And the sea arose by reason of a great wind that blew So when they had rowed about five and twenty or thirty furlongs, they see Jesus walking on the sea, and drawing nigh unto the ship: and they were afraid. But he saith unto them 'It is I. Be not afraid.' Then they willingly received him into the ship: and immediately the ship was at the land whither they went."

CHAPTER 22

Bethany

"On his arrival, Jesus found that Lazarus had already been in the tomb for four days. Now Bethany was less than two miles from Jerusalem, and many Jews had come to Martha and Mary to comfort them in the loss of their brother.....Jesus called in a loud voice, "Lazarus, come out!" The dead man came out, his hands and feet wrapped with strips of linen, and a cloth around his face. Jesus said to them, "Take off the grave clothes and let him go."

I walked out of the elevator, wiping the sleep from my eyes, wondering what breakfast would bring, and saw Paul Harris wave at me. Paul and I had met earlier on one of those many long walks up a mountain. He knew my weakness was the hills and the food.

"Good morning, sir," I said as I sat down next to him, scanning the room, hoping for a sight of pancakes and sausage.

"Good morning, Bob. Are you ready for another Middle Eastern breakfast?" Paul laughed.

I had joked to him earlier that at least I would be losing a few pounds on my journey through the Holy Land.

"What I really miss in the morning," I said, "is a nice cold glass of good, old fashioned, orange juice. Watered down Tang just does not do it for me."

Paul was having no such trouble, sampling hummus, falafel, khachapuri, challah, shakshuka, halloumi, and murtabak. I opted for a shakshuka, where I picked the tomatoes off of the egg, and grabbed a piece of banana bread. I knew I could find a Coke on the street somewhere.

Like me, Paul was writing a book. We were both on the same adventure, on our bucket lists, walking in the footprints of our Lord.

Our journey today would begin in what was then Bethany, a small village on the Mount of Olives, just a little over a mile outside of Jerusalem. Bethany was where Jesus would often stay with his friends when he was near the Holy City. Among those would have been Mary, Martha, and of course, Lazarus. Bethany seemed to be a place where Jesus could find refuge from the suddenly growing crowds. It was likely a place where he was comfortable and was treated like he was family. Luke tells us he was a frequent supper guest here.

Today Bethany is an Arab village called al-Eizariya, which is Arabic for Lazarus. We drove through what appeared to be the main street in town when I heard someone holler from the back of the bus.

"Bob! Look!"

Everyone looked out the windows. And there it was.

Hardee's.

And then the jokes started coming. Sometimes, I just make things too easy for people.

"I already had breakfast," I shouted back.

After the good natured abuse ended, we walked toward the remains of a church that was built in the 4th century, and then began our stroll through the area.

The Bethany of today is a large village, with more than 20,000 people. Street vendors were plentiful, so I had no problem finding that Coke.

I looked around and saw Paul laughing at me. I raised my can.

I walked toward a site where a group of workers were doing excavations. There was a priest from our group who was watching intently.

"Can you tell where they are digging," I asked him.

"They told me this was very near to the house of Mary, Martha and Lazarus," he said.

Once again, all you can do is look, be quiet, and wonder in amazement.

"What do you think of all these ruins?" the priest asked me.

"Amazing," I said. "Just like everything else. Amazing."

"Don't forget the other Bible stories that happened here besides Lazarus," he said. "This is where Mary anointed Jesus' feet with perfume.

BETHANY

And later Jesus ate at the home of Simon the Leper, where another woman anointed His head with a vial of perfume."

I nodded.

"Of course," he laughed, "both of those get overlooked sometimes next to raising Lazarus from the dead."

I nodded again as Anton called the group together.

"Think about what this place was like when Jesus was here," Anton said. "Two thousand years ago Bethany was a poor town. Sick people lived here. Lepers lived here. And this is where Jesus was welcome. This is where he chose to rest. This is where he chose to live his last week on earth, right alongside the broken, the needy and the sick."

"And then.......?" Anton asked the group.

"Jerusalem!" someone shouted.

"Palm Sunday," said another.

"The resurrection with the disciples," said a third.

Anton smiled. "All of the above," he said. "Come on. Let's go to the tomb."

It became impossible not to imagine what happened here more than two thousand years ago. There is a church on site with Mosaic paintings adorning the walls, telling the Lazarus story. A sign points to some steps, directing visitors to "Lazarus' Tomb" below the church.

We entered a dark cave and I slowly made my way down a staircase, with steep, slippery, rock steps. I began counting as I went down. 1-2-3-4....... there were 24 steep steps before we stopped in a small area. And then it was down some more steps to the tomb of Lazarus, where we entered in small groups because the space was so tight. There was literally no place to move. Like Jesus birth site in Bethlehem, only two people could enter at one time.

I paused and let an elderly woman enter before me.

"Shukran," she said.

I gave her my usual confused look.

"It means 'thank you'" she said.

Like many other holy sites we visited, once we arrived, there was nothing but silence among the group. Everyone took a few minutes to realize where they were, and the magnitude of what happened here, not just raising Lazarus from the dead, but everything that would soon be coming on my journey.

John told us in his gospel. "Six days before the Passover Jesus came to Bethany."

His journey, like mine, was heading toward an ending.

Indeed Jesus would be onto Jerusalem, starting with Palm Sunday. And it would end back in Bethany 40 days after his crucifixion, where Jesus would meet with his disciples, and give them their instructions to go forth into the world.

"Where you are standing," Anton told the group, "right near the home of where Mary, Martha and Lazarus lived, is the last place Jesus was ever seen on earth."

Total silence among the group.

Anton then held up his Bible. "Here is what Luke wrote about that day," he began.

"When he had led them out to the vicinity of Bethany, he lifted up his hands and blessed them. While he was blessing them, he left them and was taken up into heaven. Then they worshiped him and returned to Jerusalem with great joy. And they stayed continually at the temple, praising God."

Anton closed his Bible and walked away. The rest of us just stood, frozen, unable or unwilling to move. Finally, Anton looked back at us.

"Come on, it is lunch time," he said.

Paul had inched up next to me.

"Today's planner says we are having shawarma for lunch today Bob," he said.

I could hardly wait.

"What is it?" I asked.

"Well, it is sort of like a gyro," he said.

"Sort of?" I asked.

"Yeah," he smiled. "Try to get the chicken shawarma."

"Is there a different kind?" I asked.

"Yes," he said. "There is goat."

I just stared at him.

"I will see you on the bus," I said.

As the group dined on their shawarma's, I ventured back outside and began writing my notes. Like many other sights on my tour, the tomb of Lazarus is under Muslim rule. I thought back to the beginning of my trip to Haifa, and wondered if the Christian sights could survive the test of time. Or would someday, they have control over their own histories?

BETHANY

I looked again at the excavation going on, determined to keep checking when I get back home, year after year, to see if they found anything. I closed my notebook and began heading back.

Anton and Ayob were welcoming everyone back on the bus, making sure nobody was left behind.

"Did you enjoy the walk down to the cave today, Bob?" Anton smiled.

"I did," I said. "Shukran."

They just looked at me and laughed.

"Step up your game Bob," Ayob said. "Shukran Jazeelan."

I gave them my confused look again.

"In Arabic," Anton said. "It means thank you very much."

I got on the bus and headed toward my seat. A woman handed me a bottle of water.

"Shukran Jazeelan," I said loud enough for everyone to hear. "Shukran Jazeelan."

My little payback for the Hardee's.

"Jesus Himself suddenly stood in their midst and ... He opened their minds to understand the Scriptures ... And He led them out as far as Bethany, and He lifted up His hands and blessed them. While He was blessing them, He parted from them and was carried up into heaven......"

CHAPTER 23

The Temple of Pan

"When Jesus came to the region of Caesarea Philippi, he asked his disciples, "Who do people say the Son of Man is?" They replied, "Some say John the Baptist; others say Elijah; and still others, Jeremiah or one of the prophets." "But what about you?" he asked. "Who do you say I am?"

"The Gates of Hell"

The Temple of Pan

I have a confession to make: I had never heard of the Temple of Pan. Which was probably a good thing. I am sure it was on the high school syllabus that I had long forgotten.

As our bus rolled north, I was sitting on near Bishop A. Elias Zaidan, who was leading a group of tourists from California.

"We are going to the gates of hell," he quietly told those sitting around him. I had no idea what he meant.

We made our way through the Golan Heights. I looked out the windows and saw signs warning of Land Mines, a stark reminder of what people who live in the area deal with every day.

The bus maneuvered its way through beautiful, lush forestry, and pulled into an area surrounded by huge, beautiful orange tinged rocks. It may have been the most impressive sight I saw in the Holy Land. It was a stunning sight, with breathtaking landscaping. A postcard of God's beauty, with a 30 foot plus waterfall that fed into the Jordan River. I again paused and thought about the difficulty of the journey for Jesus and his disciples. Getting here meant dealing with hilly and rugged terrain. The area was more than a thousand feet above sea level.

And then we walked past a sign in front of a cave.

"The cave is a nucleus beside which the scared sanctuary was built. This abode of the shepherd god pagan cult began as early as the 3rd century BCE. Ritual sacrifices were cast into a natural abyss reaching underground waters at the back of the cave. If victims disappeared in the water, this was a sign that the god had accepted the offering. If however, signs of blood appeared in the nearby springs, the sacrifice had been rejected."

I stood and stared at the sign. Others gathered around me.

"What is this?" someone asked.

"They considered this the gates to the underworld," someone answered.

"Sacrifices? Are we talking about human sacrifices?" a woman asked aloud.

"Yes," another woman answered. "And most of them were infant children."

"Unbelievable," someone else said.

Legend has it the waters leading from the Cave of Pan were always colored red from the blood.

I didn't know what to say. I was just about to say to myself 'what on earth are we doing here' when I felt a strong tug at my arm. It was Diana Joseph from our group.

"Bob," she whispered, "what on earth are we doing here?"

I looked at her and just shook my head.

"I don't know," I said. "But there must be a reason."

In Greek lore, Pan was the God of the Land, the God of the Wild. He was the grandson of Zeus, and lived in the cave. He helped farmers by driving out wild animals. He was their Goliath and Samson all rolled into one.

The area is now called Banias, and it sits at the foot of Mount Hermon. Numerous earthquakes have rocked the area over centuries, including one in 1033 that collapsed most of the cave. The Temple of Pan sits carved into the cliffs of Caesarea Philippi, which was considered the most pagan place in all of Palestine. It was known as the "forbidden city." This is where the fertility gods would spend their winter.

And here, worshipers of Pan would gather and perform all sorts of unthinkable acts, from prostitution to bestiality in hopes that Pan would see their efforts and return in the spring.

Inside the cave you can still see inscriptions to Pan. I overheard a tour guide from another group say archeologists just a couple of years ago discovered nearly 50 gold coins in the area that dated to the early 600's. He told them how the city was destroyed after the war of 1967, leaving only a mosque, a church and some shrines.

Diana and I walked further up and found Bishop Zaidan.

"There," he said, pointing the group toward a cave.

"There are the Gates of Hell."

We all looked. It was a massive orange colored rock. Someone from the group pulled up a picture of Pan from their phone. A Greek god that had the upper body of a man and the legs and horns of a goat. He had wings on his back so he could fly. And he had a tail. To make matters worse, he was playing a flute.

And this is who the people of Caesarea Philippi worshiped. It was beyond belief.

I made sure Diana did not see the picture.

As we walked closer, I kept wondering how people could actually believe and worship what was in front of me. I looked around, and everyone seemed to be wondering the same thing.

Diana tugged at my arm again. "Bob, what are we doing here?"

Only one person could answer that, and on cue, the Walking Encyclopedia headed our way and spoke up.

The Temple of Pan

"You are probably wondering what we are doing here," he said, smiling, and looking at Diana. "We are here, at the Gates of Hell, because this is where Jesus took them on, right in their own backyard. This is where they would build a church that would overcome the worst among people."

Anton had everyone's full attention.

"Caesarea Philippi is the furthest spot north that Jesus brought his disciples. It was probably about a 30 mile hike for them. Imagine their shock when they arrived here, of all places. But he had a message for his disciples, and he wanted to send it to them in the darkest, baddest place possible. And the darkest, baddest place possible was the Temple of Pan. Jesus made it clear that he was not going to be intimidated by Pan, or any other false God."

Anton paused.

"And most importantly, this is where Jesus gave Peter the keys to the Kingdom of Heaven."

And now a murmur among the tourists. Heads were nodding. I knew the story from this point forward. This is where God revealed to Peter that Jesus was the Christ, the Son of the living God. I just didn't know that it happened here, in the gates of hell.

Anton looked over at Bishop Zaidan and nodded.

"People here were literally knocking on the gates of hell," the Bishop said. "Jesus then said to Peter and the other disciples, "And I tell you, you are Peter, and on this rock I will build my church, and the gates of hell shall not prevail against it.""

"Right here," Anton hollered at our group, "on this rock, sitting at the gates of hell, Jesus challenged his disciples and told them he would build his church. He wanted a church built that would overcome the worst evils. He did not want his disciples and followers running and hiding from evil. He was not afraid. Jesus wanted his disciples to know the difference between a real God, and a false one."

Anton looked around at the group.

"To Jesus, the time had come to storm the Gates of Hell."

I looked next to me at Diana, who hung on every word. Anton looked our way again.

"And for those who must have been wondering, that is why we are here today," he said.

Someone from the group asked if there were still Pagan worshipers in the area.

"Yes, but not many," Anton said. "By the fifth century, Pagan worship had basically ended. Today, there may be a couple of hundred believers. They keep to themselves. Most people probably do not even know their beliefs."

We made our way back to the bus where some of the tourists were approaching from the other direction.

"We couldn't do it," one of the women said. "Human sacrifices are too much for us."

The group instead headed for a nearby winery, and was proudly showing off their purchases.

"Avia Cabernet-Shiraz," a man said, holding up his prized possession. "A nice red wine for $35."

"Speaking of red," someone said, "did you know the water turned red here from all the blood in it?"

Some people laughed. Some did not. We got back on the bus.

Simon Peter answered, "You are the Christ, the Son of the living God." Jesus replied, "Blessed are you, Simon son of Jonah, for this was not revealed to you by man, but by my Father in heaven. And I tell you that you are Peter, and on this rock I will build my church, and the gates of Hades will not overcome it. I will give you the keys of the kingdom of heaven; whatever you bind on earth will be bound in heaven, and whatever you loose on earth will be loosed in heaven."

CHAPTER 24

Tabgha

"Bring them here to me," he said. And he directed the people to sit down on the grass. Taking the five loaves and the two fish and looking up to heaven, he gave thanks and broke the loaves. Then he gave them to the disciples, and the disciples gave them to the people. They all ate and were satisfied, and the disciples picked up twelve basketfuls of broken pieces that were left over. The number of those who ate was about five thousand men, besides women and children."

There are so many stories of miracles in the gospels. But only one, beside the resurrection, is mentioned by all four gospel writers: the feeding of the five thousand.

And what is amazing about the accounts from John, Mark, Matthew and Luke is how nearly identical they all are. The setting on top of the hill; nightfall is slowly creeping in; thousands of people are hungry; only five barley loaves remain in their baskets; next to them are only two fish. And then after Jesus blesses the little food there is, everyone eats and 12 baskets are stuffed with plenty of leftovers.

And there is probably no place in the Holy Land where we can see Jesus dealing with his disciples more so than he did that day.

The town of Tabgha sits on the northwest coast of the Sea of Galilee, on the side of the ancient river road just south of Capernaum. The land is barren. There really is no town. Very few people have ever lived here. Today the population may be a couple of hundred. They are dwarfed by the

Destination: Holy Land

thousands of visitors who flock every day to see the Church of the Multiplication, and for good reason.

They come to stand where Jesus stood and fed the masses.

Nearby is the church of Peter's Primacy. Outside the church is a sign that reads:

"The deeds and miracles of Jesus are not actions of the past. Jesus is awaiting for those who are still prepared to take risks at his word because they trust his powers utterly."

Utterly. The perfect word. Completely. Absolutely.

You spend time traveling the Holy Land, excited about seeing Bethlehem and Jerusalem, but soon realize that the most significant places in Jesus' ministry are in the Galilee area.

"Holy place. No shorts." The sign greets you upon arrival at the Multiplication Church. I hear noise, and look up and see a group of nuns ringing the church bells.

I begin taking my notes when I noticed a young man wearing a robe approaching me.

"Hello," he said. "Can I help you with any information?"

His name was Xiaohan, and he was an American college student volunteering with the German Benedictine Monastery, which oversaw the church.

"I am writing a book on the Holy Land," I told him. "I guess you could call this my bucket list."

"I have heard of those," he laughed.

"Your day will come," I told him. "In about 50 years."

We talked about life back home in America, the monastery, and then about Jesus and that little miracle before heading toward the church. I asked him about the history of the church.

"The first building built in Tabgha was right on this site, around the year 350, by Joseph of Tiberias. It was just a small chapel. Forgotten about and destroyed over time, it has been rebuilt numerous times," Xiaohan said.

Outside, in the foyer, was a large olive tree.

"It is 500 years old," Xiaohan said as I scribbled down notes.

We walked in the church and the first thing you see are the mosaic tiles on the floor.

"The original tiles," Xiaohan said.

"Original?" I asked, astonished. "From the very first church? From the year 350?"

"Yes," he said. "They are nearly 1700 years old."

I walked over the tiles, knelt down, touched them, and prayed.

"These are the earliest known Christian floor mosaics in all of the Holy Land," Xiaohan said.

As if I needed to be any more emotionally invested.

I stood up and walked to the altar. There was a basket there, with four loaves of bread and two fish on each side.

"But there were five loaves," I told Xiaohan.

"Look at Jesus," he said.

Nearby was a statue of Jesus, holding the fifth loaf of bread. I smiled. It was fantastic.

Xiaohan then told me to look under the altar.

And there was a large rock, the rock depicting where Jersus placed the loaves and fish before blessing them. Breathtaking.

Unlike the other Holy Land sites, there was very little activity here. The church had a small gift shop. Quiet and serene, I decided to walk back outside to gaze again at the Sea of Galilee, to try to remember what I was seeing now for the rest of my life. You realize that this is the place where everything started. Fishers of men. Feeding the thousands. Walking on water.

I looked down the shoreline and saw the Church of the Primacy of St. Peter, where the resurrected Jesus appeared for the fourth time and reinstated Peter as the chief of the disciples after Peter had denied him. I paused and remembered the words I had learned many years ago, as a child, in Sunday school, as Jesus spoke to Peter.

"Feed my lambs. Tend my sheep. Feed my sheep."

I pulled my small bible out of my backpack and looked for the verse. I found it in Matthew.

"And I tell you, you are Peter, and on this rock I will build my church; and the powers of death shall not prevail against it."

I looked back out onto the sea. In front of me was the living gospel, staring me in the face, a picture snapped in my mind that will last forever.

And then I looked out further, and once again found that boat I had seen earlier, empty, anchored in the water. I close my eyes and I can see it all happening. Jesus on the water, calling Peter......

Finally, my eyes drifted further, and I watched as a church group was taking communion on the shores of the Galilee. Hard to beat that moment.

I was brought back to reality by the noise behind me. Another tour group had arrived, this one from Russia. I looked at them closely. Political strangers from around the world, but brought here, today, standing beside me, looking out to the Galilee.

When their group split up to head into the church, I approached the tour guide.

"Hello," I said. "I am Bob, from America. I am writing about my journey through the Holy Land."

"I am Baruch," he said, extending his hand.

"This is a group from Russia?" I asked.

"Yes," he said.

"But you are not Russian?"

"No," he laughed. "But tour guides, we must learn many languages. I speak English and Russian, plus Hebrew and Ukrainian. You?" he asked me.

"I took French in high school," I said. "I can count to ten, but one of the numbers is missing."

He laughed again.

"Are there differences?" I asked him. "You know, tourists you see from America to tourists like your group today from Russia."

He smiled. "No differences. I had an American group last week. People love to come here. They want to be where Jesus was. Yes, they may have differences elsewhere. They may have been raised and taught differently. But when it comes to Jesus, Christians are all the same."

I nodded.

"It is time for me to catch up with my group." Baruch said.

We shook hands.

"Au revoir!" he said smiling.

And we both laughed.

"Everyone back to the bus!" Ayob awakened me with a holler. I could have stayed here forever, but I knew there were more adventures to come that day.

I walked back to the bus and heard Anton talking to the group.

"Do you know how many fish Jesus brought into the boat when he met Peter and Andrew?"

Everyone looked at each other.

"One hundred and fifty three fish," Anton said. "He filled their boat with one hundred and fifty three fish."

Xiaohan had walked up next to me.

"You should join me on the rest of the tour," I told him.

Tabgha

He laughed. "You don't need me," he said, pointing toward our tour group.

"You already have the 'Walking Encyclopedia.'"

And we both laughed.

I got on the bus and looked around. It was hot, and people were tired. We heard that a few people were forced to leave the tour due to exhaustion. And I knew as our days were dwindling, what was about to come next.

Jerusalem. The temple. The Last Supper. The Garden. The Cross. The empty tomb.

This is why I am here.

"Immediately Jesus made his disciples get into the boat and go on ahead of him to Bethsaida, while he dismissed the crowd. After leaving them, he went up on a mountainside to pray."

CHAPTER 25

Jerusalem

"O Jerusalem, Jerusalem, thou that killest the prophets, and stonest them which are sent unto thee, how often would I have gathered thy children together, even as a hen gathereth her chickens under her wings, and ye would not!"

"The girl with the gun"

Jerusalem

As our bus pulled into the hotel, Ayob stood up to speak.

"Your dinner menu tonight will include Hashweh, Shish Tawook, and Musakhan."

Of course, by now, everyone just looked at me and laughed.

"And prepare yourselves," Ayob said. "Because tomorrow we go to Jerusalem."

I looked around. Nobody was laughing now. Everyone knew what lie ahead. I laid in bed that night and just stared at the darkness. My mind started racing one at a time. On Wednesday he was overthrowing the temple. Thursday was the last supper, Judas, the Garden of Gethsemane, the arrest, Peter, Pilate. Friday would bring The Way of the Cross, and then of course Calvary.

And then Sunday.

The Resurrection.

Sleep was not coming. In the darkness I prayed, prayed that I could handle everything, prayed that I could remember everything. I watched the minutes on the clock roll by. I was in and out of sleep now. And then there was light, and I jumped out of bed.

I had gotten to know many of the people in our group by now. They had come from all corners of America, all united in their pursuit to see this land, one time in their life before it was too late. I suspected they had all been unable to sleep, staring at the darkness, just like me.

How would I handle things in Jerusalem? I had no idea. But I would bring two pairs of sunglasses, with pockets stuffed with kleenex.

At the breakfast table the others were again quiet. It was as if all the moments up until now were fantastic, but this…….this was a whole other level of emotion.

There was still very little talking on the bus. Finally, Ayob stood up.

"We have to go through a checkpoint to enter Jerusalem," he said. "Do not worry. It is like a toll booth in America. But I have to get off the bus and tell the guard who we are."

The bus stopped and I looked out the window as Ayob talked to the guard, who turned to look at the bus.

She was a teenager carrying a rifle.

I was clearly in a different world now. I knew Jerusalem was going to be a love-hate relationship with me.

As I stepped off the bus and onto the sacred ground of Jerusalem, I said out loud to myself what I whisper to myself all the time.

I am a disciple of Jesus Christ.

There was a tug at my arm.

"I am keeping my eyes on you today, Bob."

It was Delores Koury, the one with the K, the one pushing 90, which was surely more than she weighed.

"We've got this," she said, clutching my hand.

I nodded, and off we strolled.

We looked around and I thought about Jesus, and what he must have thought in his final days. Surely he was convinced that he had to take his message to Jerusalem. He surely knew of the city's history of killing prophets, including John the Baptist. And I closed my eyes and pictured his triumphant arrival on Palm Sunday, riding into the city on a donkey. There is no doubt that once he overthrew the temple, and challenged the authorities, he knew his life was in danger.

"Bob?" Delores nudged me. "What are you thinking? I can tell your mind in wondering"

We smiled at each other.

"Just wishing I could have been here 2,000 years ago," I said, as we continued our walk into the city.

After World War I, Christian's made up roughly 20 percent of the population in Jerusalem. Today, the number is two percent, and falling. In one of the world's great cities, with a population pushing one million, and with so much Christian tradition, only about 15,000 Christians now call Jerusalem home.

For many Christians, local Israeli radical groups have made their lives unbearable via hate crimes. Christian families have watched as militant groups have moved into their once safe neighborhoods. It is likely the number of Christians in the spiritual capital of the world will continue to shrink, and eventually become a footnote to history, and the Christian footprint in Jerusalem will be nothing more than a museum.

I stopped to buy a drink at a small shop.

"Good morning," I said to the man behind the counter.

"Good morning," he answered.

"My name is Bob. I am writing a book on my travels through the Holy Land."

He said his name was Tamar, and his family had operated the store for more than 20 years. I asked him how times had changed with the Christian population.

"Christians? They are mostly just visitors now," he said. "And mostly my customers," he smiled. "Very few of them actually live here."

We talked for a few minutes about where I had been, what I would see in Jerusalem, and then about Christianity and Judaism, and how people of different faiths got along in the Old City.

"I really think Jewish people get along with Christians here," he said. "People are courteous. Nobody is looking for problems. But, it's not like with the Jews and the Muslims. They will never get along."

I mentioned how much our faiths have in common, and how in America, Christians and Jews mingle constantly, sometimes in interfaith gatherings.

"Yes," Tamar said. "Good people are good people. But here, it is mainly all Jews except for the tourists."

I thanked him for the drink, and he smiled.

"Would you like to sign my wall, Mister Bob?"

I glanced at his wall that had numerous signatures.

"To my friend Tamar," I wrote. "We have much in common, Bob."

We shook hands and said goodbye. A very nice 10 minutes of my life.

I caught back up with Delores and we looked out over the city.

"It really is beautiful," she said.

I nodded.

She looked at me and asked, "what are you thinking about this time, Bob?"

I just gazed ahead. I couldn't even speak. But I was thinking. The Temple. The Last Supper. The Garden of Gethsemane. The Way of the Cross. Calvary.

The Resurrection.

How was I ever going to get through it?

I snapped out of it when I heard Ayob call the group.

"We will be sight seeing for a little bit. You can see the city and do some shopping. Our first stop later will be the churches. Enjoy them. Things might get more difficult for you after that."

And with that I put one foot in front of the other and moved on with my eyes wide opened. I wanted to see it all. And I remembered the words of Luke as Jesus entered Jerusalem on Palm Sunday.

"As he approached Jerusalem and saw the city, he wept over it."

I saw some of our group walking ahead, and I caught up with them.

"Where are we going?" I asked.

"Arab Souq," a man said.

"What?" I asked.

"It's an Arab market," he said. "You will find some cool items here."

We were in the midst of the Christian and Muslim Quarters. It was a winding collection of alleyways selling everything. Each "store" was incredibly small, and as I kept walking and counting, I thought there must have been a thousand of them, most selling the same thing.

The first item that intrigued me was a tee shirt that read "I don't need Google. My wife knows everything."

As the others shopped, one of the women hollered at me.

"Bob, this way!"

She pulled me into a place called Jaffar Sweets.

"How did you know?" I asked, smiling.

We walked in and I asked the woman behind the counter what she reccommended.

"You must try knafeh," she said. "Ours is the best in Jerusalem."

I looked at the woman who dragged me into this.

"We will take two," I said, wondering what I had gotten myself into.

"Hot or cold?" I was asked.

I shrugged my shoulders. The woman I was with had the answer.

"Give us one of each," she said.

Our knafeh came looking like a large slice of pie, filled with a sweet tasting cheese, topped with syrup. It was crispy, and yes, it was good. Like, really, really good.

With a full belly we headed back toward our group. There were amazing churches awaiting us. And then things would really get real.

"And I saw the holy city, new Jerusalem, coming down out of heaven from God, prepared as a bride adorned for her husband. And I heard a loud voice from the throne saying, "Behold, the dwelling place of God is with man. He will dwell with them, and they will be his people, and God himself will be with them as their God."

CHAPTER 26

The Churches

"Jesus was praying in a certain place, and after he had finished, one of his disciples said to him, "Lord, teach us to pray, as John taught his disciples."

He said to them, "When you pray, say:
    Father, hallowed be your name.
    Your kingdom come.
    Give us each day our daily bread
    and forgive us our sins,
    for we ourselves forgive everyone indebted to us.
    And do not bring us to the final test."

"Church, then spaghetti!"

"Today we are visiting many churches," Anton told the group. "You will see the greatest churches you have ever seen. It will prepare you for the days to come."

Our first stop was the churches sitting atop the Mount of Olives. You have to understand the history of the area. Most of the events centered around Jesus' life happened near the Mount, while the most important Jewish cemetery in the world is here, with nearly 100,000 graves. Muslim tombs are here. It is essentially a mountain top of churches, cemeteries and mosques. Christians, Jews and Muslims all gather here on pilgrimages, as the Mount gives the clearest view for all faiths of the Temple Mount below. Visitors have been flocking to the area for centuries. Perhaps nowhere else in the world are the three faiths so closely gathered, or as some would say, so closely contested.

Much of the final days of Jesus' life are centered here; his arrival in Jerusalem on Palm Sunday, the Last Supper, Crucifixion and Resurrection. Christians, Jews and Muslims all believe the end of days is going to happen right here.

Anton gathered us as we headed toward our first church, the Church of the Pater Noster, also known as the Church of Our Father.

"At one time, there were roughly 25 Christian churches here," he told us. "It was basically its own city."

The first thing you notice walking in are the languages, nearly 200 of them, writing the Lord's Prayer on the walls. Underneath the church, near the summit of the Mount, is a cave where Jesus would have taught his disciple the prayer above.

"This is one of the earliest churches built," Anton said. "It dates to the fourth century. It must be considered one of the holiest sites in the world."

I looked for the English version written on the walls. And there I found the gospel of Matthew, chapter 6, verse 14.

"For if you forgive other people when they sin against you, your heavenly Father will also forgive you. But if you do not forgive others their sins, your Father will not forgive your sins."

Anton waved us all together.

"This was the first time Jesus used the phrase 'Our Father.'"

Our next stop was the Church of All Nations, also known as the Basilica of the Agony, built over a rock where Jesus prayed the night before he was crucified. The church standing today is about 100 years old, believed to be the third church built on site. Before entering, you pass through the garden of olive trees. There are 12 domes atop the church commemorating the 12 nations who helped build it, and there are parts of the mosaic floor from the original church that are under glass and may be seen in the floor. The church has a dark feel to it, meant to give the feeling of Jesus praying at night, with olive branches hanging nearby, just as they do in the Garden of Gethsemane, sitting next door.

Ah, the garden. I kept looking. It was calling me. But it had to wait for another day.

You walk into the church, and there in the front of the altar is The Rock.

I waited my turn as I watched Tony and Marybeth Couri walked up to the rock before me. We had become seat buddies on the daily bus rides, and thus shared the daily experience of expectations, reality, and then exaltation afterwards. I watched them knowing they were thinking the same thing I was.

The Rock. The site where Jesus kneeled and prayed before he was arrested.

Nearby stood a statue of Luke, holding a book, with the inscription "And being in an agony he prayed more earnestly; and his sweat became like great drops of blood falling down to the ground."

People were surrounding the rock. Many were kneeling. Some were touching. Tears were flowing. I watched as Tony and Marybeth finished, then turned back and looked at me. Tony nodded. Marybeth tried to smile, but the emotions were raw. I made my way to the altar. It is just hard to keep describing where your mind goes in those few, sacred minutes.

A couple of years before we arrived, archaeologists discovered a 1,500 year old bath site near the church, with the inscription "for the memory and repose of those who love Christ….."

That would be me. And Tony and Marybeth. I couldn't wait to get back on the bus and talk about it.

And then we were onto the Dormition Church. It is impossible to miss, one of the most striking in the city, with a huge dome that dominates the Jerusalem skyline. This may be where Mary died. Or it may have been thousands of miles away. Early traditions point to Jerusalem, here, at the Tomb of Mary, at the foot of the Mount of Olives. But on the cross, Jesus said to John, "behold your mother." And John built his church in Ephesus, modern day Turkey, and there is a home there claiming to be Mary's.

The Dormition Church has a beautiful mosaic of Mary and the infant Jesus. Underneath is the inscription from Isaiah 7:14; "Behold, a virgin shall conceive, and bear a son, and shall call his name Immanuel."

In the middle of the church is a statue of Mary, sleeping in death. Above her are other women from the old testament: Ruth, Esther, Judith, Eve, Miriam and Jael.

I pulled Anton aside.

"Jerusalem or Ephesus?" I asked.

The Walking Enclyclopedia went with Jerusalem. I shook my head.

"I am going with Ephesus," I said. "John would have never left her behind."

Anton smiled. "It is certainly possible," he said.

Jerusalem or Ephesus makes no difference to me. This is the Virgin Mary, the mother of our Lord and Savior. My heart is full.

Back on the bus, Ayob spoke to the group. I think we were all prepared for what was coming next.

"Get some rest," he told us. "Tomorrow is the day."

We were heading to the Last Supper. And my journey into the Garden. The garden that I stared at as our bus pulled out. The garden that I had long dreamed of stepping into and praying. So close now I could touch it.

We were ushered back to our rooms. I looked over again and saw Marybeth.

"Dinner tonight, Bob?" she asked.

"I will probably pass again," I said.

I laid down to rest in my room when the phone call came.

"Bob, get down here right this minute!" Ilda Couri was hollering at me.

"Ilda," I said, "you know I can't eat that food!"

"Bob, it's spaghetti! Real spaghetti!"

I hung up the phone, and made it down three levels of stairs in near record time.

Spaghetti never tasted so good.

Sitting next to me, Lolly Maroon could not stop smiling.

"I have never seen anyone eat so fast," she said.

"Well, it has been a few days," I said between mouthfuls.

The rest of the table was hooting and hollering, enjoying my sudden appetite.

"Slow down Bob," Aggie Couri said. "This is not your last supper!"

I really could not remember when my last supper was. But noodles, with something resembling red sauce, was good enough.

"Can you ask them to bring me some parmesan cheese?" I asked the group. "And maybe some garlic bread?"

And everyone laughed.

Eventually, they either ran out of spaghetti, or I finished, and our group talked about what was coming. We would revisit Thursday night with Jesus. That meant the Last Supper, then a trip to the Garden of Gethsemane. By now, everyone knew the garden trip was atop my bucket list, and by now, they knew how much I would struggle with it.

"Make sure you get a good night's sleep Bob," Gretta Couri told me, smiling, knowing full well that would be impossible.

"At least you can sleep on a full stomach," Lolly laughed.

There would be little sleep. I had dreamt of this moment for years. To be in the Last Supper room? To be in the Garden of Gethsemane? To venture into the courtyard where Jesus stood before Pilate? To see where he was flogged and beaten? How does one prepare for those moments? How does one sleep?

For me, the answer was hardly at all. Not even with a full stomach.

"When you pray, do not be like the hypocrites, for they love to pray standing in the synagogues and on the street corners to be seen by men ... but when you pray, go into your room, close the door and pray to your father who is unseen."

CHAPTER 27

The Last Supper

"When evening came, Jesus was reclining at the table with the Twelve. And while they were eating, he said, "Truly I tell you, one of you will betray me." They were very sad and began to say to him one after the other, "Surely you don't mean me, Lord? Jesus replied, "The one who has dipped his hand into the bowl with me will betray me. The Son of Man will go just as it is written about him. But woe to that man who betrays the Son of Man! It would be better for him if he had not been born." Then Judas, the one who would betray him, said, "Surely you don't mean me, Rabbi?" Jesus answered, "You have said so."

"Surely you don't mean me, Rabbi?"

The Last Supper

Time for full disclosure: Among all the strange traits that define me, and there are far too many to disclose here, perhaps none is more bizarre than what is in my head as I am walking around attempting to be a normal human being.

I silently sing to myself. Just a handful of the lines, over and over and over. And as we rode the bus this morning, in quiet, to the Upper Room where Jesus held the Last Supper, my head was working overtime, which meant the lyrics were flowing.

> *"King of Kings and Lord of Lords, and he shall reign forever and ever. Hallelujah! Hallelujah!"*

I kept my eyes closed. This was my time, and I needed to spend it alone. I knew what this day was going to mean to me. The Last Supper, followed by the Garden of Gethsemane. We were heading to the cross and the end of my journey with Jesus.

The bus came to a stop and I looked around. The Gospels have little information about the location of the Last Supper, just a vague reference to an "upper room." What stands today as the likely site is a three story structure atop King David's tomb, hosting a synagogue, which means it is a holy site to Muslims, Jews and Christians. Pilgrims began visiting the site in the 4th century, and the current building was renovated in the 1300's. Some Christian theologians believe the upper room was the very first location of a Christian church.

I walked inside with a lifetime snapshot in my mind: the Hollywood movies; the da Vinci painting. And it was nothing like that.

The room is in the second story of a chapel. It is rectangular, large, and open. It was crowded with tourists, and had a quiet and somber feel. It felt cold. It felt new, as if it could have passed for any office building, not something 700 years old. The present building was built in the 12th century. There were Gothic arches on the vaulted ceiling above us and stone floors below. There are stained glass windows with Arabic inscriptions. I looked around for something special to remember the room by, but felt nothing. There were no ornaments, or anything memorializing the Last Supper. It was just a large, barren, dark, cold room that looked like hundreds you could see on any day in America. In a word, it was sterile. The only thing that stood out in the room was an olive tree with three trunks, symbolizing peace between Christians, Jews and Muslims.

As centuries have rolled on, the site has been renovated multiple times and controlled by various groups. Christians were banned from visiting for 400 years, finally ending in 1948 when Israel took control of the building.

The best you could do was close your eyes and turn back the clock 2,000 years. Where is the spot where Jesus would have washed Peter's feet? Where did the table sit? What about the bread our Lord dipped into wine? Where is the side door where Judas snuck out? There were no answers. Just a large empty room.

Of course, that did not stop me.

> *"King of Kings and Lord of Lords, and he shall reign forever and ever. Hallelujah! Hallelujah!"*

I pictured a long table, filled with fish and bread, wine and dates. There sat Jesus in the middle, Peter on one side, John on the other. Judas was there.

> *"King of Kings and Lord of Lords, and he shall reign forever and ever. Hallelujah! Hallelujah!"*

It was a letdown. I suddenly longed for da Vinci's beautiful painting. There was Bartholomew, James and Andrews on the left; Judas is tipping over the salt, holding his money bag, next to Peter, who looks angry, and is whispering to John; Jesus sits in the middle; then Thomas who has his finger in the air, as if he doubts something, sitting next to James the Greater, and Philip; Matthew, Thaddeus and Simon the Zealot are on the far right.

Leonardo da Vinci painted the Last Supper just before 1500. Remarkably, he painted the Mona Lisa just a few years later. Today the Last Supper hangs in a museum in Italy, widely considered the most important mural painting in the world, one the richest person in the world could not buy.

It is priceless. And its image stands forever.

I looked around at the other tourists, and I could see by the looks on their faces that they felt the same way that I did. I ventured toward another tour group, and saw a woman shaking her head.

"Not exactly the upper room that you were hoping for?" I asked.

"No, not at all," she said. "Not even close. Certainly not like the one I have seen portrayed in the movies. Or the paintings."

"Hollywood," I said. "And da Vinci. But we know they got some things wrong."

She looked at me.

The Last Supper

"Well they always depict the disciples as older men. We know they were much younger."

She laughed. She said her name was Amy and she was with a tour group from Dallas. We discovered her group was following the same schedule as ours today.

"I'm just going to block this room from my mind," she said. "and go back to my memory. To me, the Last Supper is that painting in that quaint little room. It is what I have seen in the movies. It is certainly not this."

I agreed. I reminded her that the Garden of Gethsemane was coming up later today for both of us.

"Now that......," I began to tell her.

"Will be the real thing.......," she finished and laughed.

"Unless they found a new garden......," I said.

"Maybe that was a new Sea of Galilee we saw......" she said.

We paused.

"That old boat they found," I finally said.

"What about the boat with no anchor?" she asked.

"And the Fishers of Men," I said.

We looked back at the Last Supper Room.

"Just not much to see here," she said.

I agreed and everyone began heading out.

We then heard noise, and realized people around us had begun singing. It had become common now on the streets of Jerusalem, Christian visitors singing worship hymns.

"Are you a singer?" Amy asked me.

I could only laugh. If she only knew. I gave her a small sample.

"King of Kings and Lord of Lords, and he shall reign forever and ever! Hallelujah! Hallelujah!"

Then I thanked her for not laughing.

We walked out the door together. The upper room may have been a disappointment, but I knew the Garden of Gethsemane was just around the corner. I spotted my tour group again.

"Thoughts?" I asked them.

I saw long faces and shaking of heads. Their experience was just like mine and Amy's.

"It is okay," I told them. "Keep the pictures you have in your mind forever."

We watched and listened as more carolers paraded through the streets. When they finished their song I hollered out.

"Sing King of Kings!"

They looked our way, gathered in a circle for a minute, and then they began.

> "King of Kings and Lord of Lords, and he shall reign forever and ever! Hallelujah! Hallelujah!"

It was slightly better than my version.

"Bob!" I turned and looked. It was Diana Joseph. She knew. My group all knew by now what this was about to mean to me.

"Gethsemane, Bob," Diana said, pulling my arm. "We are going to Gethsemane. It is your time."

I tried to smile and we began the slow walk. And I prepared myself for the moment of a lifetime.

"While they were eating, Jesus took bread, and when he had given thanks, he broke it and gave it to his disciples, saying, "Take and eat; this is my body." Then he took a cup, and when he had given thanks, he gave it to them, saying, "Drink from it, all of you. This is my blood of the[covenant, which is poured out for many for the forgiveness of sins. I tell you, I will not drink from this fruit of the vine from now on until that day when I drink it new with you in my Father's kingdom."

CHAPTER 28

The Grotto of Gethsemane

Then Jesus went with his disciples to a place called Gethsemane, and he said to them, "Sit here while I go over there and pray." He took Peter and the two sons of Zebedee along with him, and he began to be sorrowful and troubled. Then he said to them, "My soul is overwhelmed with sorrow to the point of death. Stay here and keep watch with me."

"Stay here and keep watch with me."

Destination: Holy Land

I could see the garden from a distance as I began the slow walk down the steps toward it. We are at the foot of the Mount of Olives. In the distance was the Old City, with the Dome of the Rock hovering above Jerusalem, the city of David, the temple built by Solomon, the site where Jesus was crucified, buried and resurrected. It is both breathtaking and heartbreaking. It is impossible to look at it and not see everything, all at once. And then to picture what Jesus saw when he looked into the distance that night in the garden. He would have seen the same ancient, giant olive trees that were everywhere. Trees that may have gone back thousands of years.

Above the entrance is a sign with the spelling Getsemani, with four crosses surrounding it. I paused before walking in. Somewhere, right near where I was standing, is where Judas would have betrayed Jesus with a kiss. As you enter, there is a sign describing the biblical events that occurred here.

At the entrance of the garden is the Grotto of Gethsemane, where Jesus asked Peter, John and James to stay and wait for him while he prayed. And here we see Jesus not just as our Savior, but as one of us, a mere human, with frailties.

I thought back to Cana, and turning the water into wine miracle as I opened the gate and ventured inside. Jesus knew then that his day had not yet come. "Woman, why do you involve me?" he told Mary. "My hour has not yet come." But he knew on this night that indeed his time had come. And as any of us would be, he was scared. And in the small garden, his disciples could hear him as he prayed.

"My father, if there is any way, get me out of this. Take this cup from me."

Yes, our Lord was afraid. He was just like us, in complete human form. None of us know when our time will come. But Jesus knew his time was at hand the minute he dipped his bread and gave it to Judas. "What you are about to do, do quickly," he told him. So Jesus knew that whatever was about to happen, it was about to happen that night.

You go into a small cave in the garden called the Cave of the Betrayal, in reference to Judas, and realize how small it is. My first impression was that it looked ancient, as old as anything I had seen in the Holy Land. There was hardly a touch of remodeling here. It is located just outside the entrance to where they claim Mary's tomb is. You go down the steps to the grotto and there is an altar with pieces of art showing Jesus praying with his disciples. Next to them is a picture of Judas kissing Jesus. There are water paintings on walls, faded, but beautiful. The cave has rarely been altered over generations, except for its entrance and a modern stone floor. Archeologists believe it was once used as an olive press. A water cistern discovered after a flood in the cave in 1955 dates before Jesus' time and sits nearby.

"This grotto is very likely a spot where the disciples spent many nights," Anton told our group. "This was a place where Jesus prayed at night. It would have been a convenient resting spot. And it was on the path between Jerusalem and Bethany, places where Jesus and his followers spent much if their time. And is a likely spot where Jesus may have met Nicodemus. Before Jesus time, this was likely an old oil mill. After Jesus time, farmers would store their grain here. And it has been used as a cemetery."

I pulled out my small bible and turned to Matthew.

"Then he returned to his disciples and found them sleeping. "Couldn't you men keep watch with me for one hour?" he asked Peter. "Watch and pray so that you will not fall into temptation. The spirit is willing, but the flesh is weak."

That line, "the spirit is willing, but the flesh is weak," would sum up not just what Jesus thought about his disciples sleeping, but also what was happening within his spirit, and his flesh. He was willing, but he knew the pain that was soon to come.

There are faded murals in the wall of the grotto. I got as close as I could and read the inscription.

"Sustinete Hic Et Vigilate Mecum."

A man standing next to me saw that I was struggling as I wrote it down. "It is Latin," he said. "It means 'Stay here and keep watch with me.'"

We both then looked down at the sculptures of Jesus praying with the disciples. I watched as the man shook his head.

"They kept falling asleep," he said. "Can you imagine falling asleep in the presence of Jesus?"

I can only smile and nod. I could not speak if I wanted to. We were both in that moment.

We moved along and came to other inscriptions. The man with me had a book that did the translations.

"That one says 'Christ the Savior frequented this place with his disciples.'"

We nudged our way to another.

"It says 'My Father, if it is your wish, let this chalice pass from me,'" the man read.

And then finally, we found one more. He read the words slowly.

"Here, the King sweated blood."

We both paused and stared at the words.

"Excuse me," he said. And I watched as he walked to some nearby seats where others were sitting and praying. I saw tears in his eyes, and I realized in this moment, I was not alone. You stand here, and you understand that nothing else in the world matters.

Jesus walked back into the garden, and knelt again.

"My Father, if there is no other way than this, drinking this cup to the dregs, I am ready. Do it your way."

If there was ever a doubt in Jesus' mind about what was about to come, it had ended.

Among all the sites I saw in the Holy Land, this grotto, this cave, the Cave of the Betrayal, stands among the holiest sites because of its original appearance. This, among all sites, screamed life at Jesus' time. This small ancient cave would have been the type of cave Jesus was born in back in Bethlehem. This would have been what it looked like when Joseph and Mary had to flee and hide with Baby Jesus from Herod. This is how I pictured Jesus teaching his disciples, and then them sleeping for the night.

In a place just like this.

"All the tourists come to the garden," Anton told our group. "But for some reason, many of them skip the grotto."

What a shame I thought. What a shame.

As we headed out of the grotto, I spotted the man who read me the Latin. He waved me over.

"Sorry about that," he said. "I just had me a moment. I'm Jim."

"Well Jim," I said, "keep an eye on me. We are about to head into the garden. If anybody is about to have a moment, it is me."

We both laughed. In a few minutes, those laughs would be tears.

I found my group waiting outside the grotto. They were interested in what I had translated from the inscriptions.

"You mean you don't speak Latin?" I asked.

"And neither do you," someone hollered. "We heard you can't even count to ten in French!"

They had me there. I went over the translations with them.

"Stay here and keep watch with me."

"Christ the Savior frequented this place with his disciples."

"My Father, if it is your wish, let this chalice pass from me."

The Grotto of Gethsemane

"Here, the King sweated blood."

And then the group became quiet. Anton approached us.

"Who is ready to go into the Garden of Gethsemane?"

Everyone looked at me.

"Bob?" Anton asked.

I nodded. I thought about that second pair of sunglasses in my backpack. I knew the Catholics on the trip would be going inside the church on site for mass. I knew that would give me time, alone, in the garden.

Exactly why I was here.

"When he came back, he again found them sleeping, because their eyes were heavy. So he left them and went away once more and prayed the third time, saying the same thing. Then he returned to the disciples and said to them, "Are you still sleeping and resting?"

CHAPTER 29

The Garden of Gethsemane

"And going a little farther, he fell on the ground and prayed that, if it were possible, the hour might pass from him. And he said, "Abba, Father, all things are possible for you. Remove this cup from me. Yet not what I will, but what you will."

"A cloud, a bird, and my Savior"

The Garden of Gethsemane

Just steps from the grotto where the disciples fell asleep, and there I was, staring at the number one thing on my bucket list site, the place I always dreamt of seeing more than any place in the world.

The Garden of Gethsemane.

By now, the people who made this trip halfway around the world with me knew what this moment, among all moments, meant to me. I did my best to look at each of them, to remember their faces and to never forget this day. There was Gretta walking with Delores, both watching me; Lolly and Aggie were together, waving; Tony and Marybeth smiled at me; Ilda and Diana could hardly contain themselves.

"Bob, you are here!" they hollered. "You made it!"

And then I felt a tug at my arm.

"See it, remember it, write it." It was Gene Couri, a mentor on the trip. "I can't wait to read it. And don't worry. I've got the pictures."

Gene's camera never left his neck during the trip. My memory might wane, but not today. Never would I forget what was about to happen today.

The church bells started ringing loudly above us. People were pouring out of tour buses. But instead of coming to the garden, they were rushing into the nearby Church of the Gethsemane for noon mass. My group began heading in and waved back at me.

"Enjoy it Bob," Gene said as he headed toward church. "It's all yours."

And then suddenly, there I was, alone, standing in the place of my dreams. My mind was whirling in silence.

> ".....I come to the garden alone
> While the dew is still on the roses
> And the voice I hear, falling on my ear
> The Son of God discloses....."

Where to begin?

There is a plaque on the gate that says "This site is dedicated exclusively to prayer."

The garden is humble, smaller than I had anticipated. Surely small enough that Peter, John and James could have heard Jesus praying before they fell asleep, and their stories in the Bible are incredibly similar.

I look around and I see giant olive trees, birds hopping among the branches. I look up and I see the Dome of the Rock. There is one small cloud in the sky, sitting directly over my head. I smile. He is watching me.

> *"…..And He walks with me*
> *And He talks with me*
> *And He tells me I am His own*
> *And the joy we share as we tarry there*
> *None other has ever known….."*

I have been asked what it felt like. The only word that comes to mind is overwhelming. To me, this is where the most emotional moment in the Bible took place, thousands of years ago. Jesus comes here to take upon his shoulders not only every sin that has ever been committed, but every sin that ever will be. Your sins, my sins. Our great grandchildren's sins. In this garden, where I now stood, he made the choice to drink from a cup that he did not deserve. He showed his human side here, scared, knowing what was about to come. He wanted the cup taken away.

The exact location of Gethsemane, like many other ancient Biblical sites, is unknown. It mattered little to me as I began my walk amongst the olive trees, quiet except for birds singing with me.

> *"…..He speaks and the sound of His voice*
> *Is so sweet the birds hush their singing*
> *And the melody that He gave to me*
> *Within my heart is ringing….."*

The garden is a grove of olive trees that includes about eight what appear to be very old, very large trees, most of them hundreds of years old, possibly some of them thousands, which means……..

That my Lord and Savior may have knelt and prayed beside one of these trees before me, as they regrow from their roots after dying. My head started spinning, looking for the oldest trees that I could find. And then I needed one that would have looked toward the Old City, surely as Jesus would have done that night. I went from tree to tree to tree, narrowing my list. I had eight options, then cut it to two. I could not separate them.

And then a bird landed on one right in front of me. I smiled and looked up at the cloud.

"Okay," I said. "I got it."

> *"….And He walks with me*
> *And He talks with me*
> *And He tells me I am His own*
> *And the joy we share as we tarry there*
> *None other has ever known…."*

The Garden of Gethsemane

I knelt by the fence just outside the tree. I looked at the city. I looked at the bird and the cloud. And then it all came pouring out. Just a lifetime of guilt, wondering if I had done enough, if I had believed enough, if I fell way short in God's eyes. And then suddenly it all changed, and I felt tears of joy. I prayed and I laughed and I cried all at the same time. My head was spinning. I never wanted to leave. I remember thinking, "I am glad Catholic masses go on so long."

Because the Garden of Gethsemane was mine, and mine alone.

> "....I stayed in the garden with Him
> Though the night all around me is falling
> But He bids me go, through the voice of woe
> His voice to me is calling....."

A young priest came walking my way. I stand up, try to gather myself, and he smiled.

"Hello," he says. "I am Father Diego Gassa. Welcome to the garden. I see you found the tree."

I looked back at the tree and him.

"This is probably our oldest tree. This might be the spot where Jesus knelt to pray. How did you pick this tree?"

"A little birdie told me," I said, and we both laughed.

Father Gassa was part of the Franciscan Friars, a group in charge of watching over and tending to the garden.

"How long have you been watching over the garden?" I asked.

"About 12 years," he said.

I smiled. "This must be the greatest job in the world."

"It has its remarkable benefits," he laughed.

We talked about my journey, and how important the garden visit was to me. We talked about his journey from Italy to the garden.

"The garden is where you stay with Jesus," he said. "And when you stay with Jesus, you discover God."

Father Gassa looked at his watch.

"Mass will be ending in a few minutes," he said. "I think I will leave you a few more minutes by yourself."

We shook hands. And I knelt again.

Would I ever be in a holy place like this again? I knew the walk up Calvary was coming. I knew there would be the heartbreak of a cross, and then the exaltation of an empty tomb. But this.....this was prayer. This is what I do every night, alone in the dark, in my bed. To do it here, where

Jesus did, under this tree, with a bird tweeting next to me and a cloud still above me.......

I paused and thought, "Where in the world would I rather be than right here, right now?

And the answer was nowhere.

I began to hear noises and looked up. More tour buses were arriving. The church bells were ringing. Mass was ending. I looked to the sky once more, and my cloud was now gone. I turned and looked for my bird. Gone. It was time to go. My group came rushing out.

"Bob!' Gretta waved. There was Ilda and Diana, Tony and Marybeth, Lolly and Aggie. And finally Gene, helping escort Delores down the steps, one eye on her, one on me.

"That was a beautiful mass," Delores said. "Bob, you should have come inside."

Gene looked at me and smiled. "I think Bob did just fine, Delores."

Others from the group soon followed, and I watched them walk through the garden, looking at the magnificent old olive trees. Soon the garden was packed. I watched people kneel as best they could with the crowd and pray. They were having a wonderful moment. But it could not have matched mine.

When I left the garden, I took the tree, the cloud and the bird with me. They stay forever.

"....And He walks with me
And He talks with me
And He tells me I am His own
And the joy we share as we tarry there
None other has ever known
None other has ever known...."

"Look, the hour has come, and the Son of Man is delivered into the hands of sinners. Rise! Let us go! Here comes my betrayer!"

CHAPTER 30

Gallicantu

"While he was still speaking, Judas, one of the Twelve, arrived, accompanied by a large crowd, with swords and clubs, who had come from the chief priests and the elders of the people. His betrayer had arranged a sign with them, saying, "The man I shall kiss is the one; arrest him." Immediately he went over to Jesus and said, "Hail, Rabbi!"* and he kissed him. Jesus answered him, "Friend, do what you have come for." Then stepping forward they laid hands on Jesus and arrested him.

"The Rooster Crows"

And then we were off to Gallicantu, to Caiaphas and Peter, to Pilate and Barabbas. A place where a question lurked in my mind that had bothered me for years.

Gallicantu in Latin means "the Rooster Crows." And on that night, the rooster crowed three times as Jesus was brought into the courtyard, the house of the High Priest Caiaphas. Of course, the rooster was crowing for Peter.

Outside the church, in the courtyard is a statue telling the story of the denial. There is Peter, a woman, a roman soldier, and a rooster. The inscription underneath says "But he denied him, saying "Woman, I know him not!"

As I walked in and looked around I tried to imagine Peter that night. He not only denied knowing Jesus three times, he ran away. Like all the other disciples except John, he was a no-show at the cross. But here is the thing: Peter denied knowing Jesus just knowing that Jesus was arrested. He certainly didn't know Jesus was about to be beaten and crucified. Nor did the others. But they fled, just on the arrest. Imagine if they knew what was to come. And Peter, among all of them, was "the rock." The strong one.

But not that night. And not the next day.

The first church was built on this site in the 5th century. Today, a modern church sits on the site, the Church of Saint Peter in Gallicantu, built in 1931. North of the church is a very old staircase leading down to the Kidron Valley, surely the same path Jesus would have walked from his arrest in Gethsemane to the courtyard. The first thing you notice is the roof of the church, where a golden rooster sits atop a black cross.

At the entrance of the church is a statue of Jesus, bound. You walk inside and see marble columns and arch windows, and a beautiful ceiling with a huge cross shaped window of various colors. In the middle of the sanctuary there is a hole where you can see caves with walls adorned with crosses from centuries ago.

"Those crosses date back to the 5th century," Anton told us.

And there, underneath the main sanctuary, 2,000 years comes to life. I looked at the group around me. I think everyone knew this was going to be a difficult moment.

A sign pointed us downward. "One way crypt blessed sacrament. Chapel courtyard and holy stairs. Sacred pit. Dungeon."

It felt like we were walking into a haunted house. We made our way down the ancient steps.

"What you are looking at down here are multiple caves," Anton told our group. "They date back to the second temple, so what does this mean?"

We looked at the caves, and each other. And it sunk in. This is where Jesus would have been imprisoned.

"Come this way," Anton told us. "Now look up."

There was a manhole above us.

"Jesus would have been lowered down through that hole, into a dungeon cell."

You look around, and realize you are standing in the ultimate house of horrors. This is where Jesus would have been beaten and flogged. I thought back to years ago, when I had gone to the theatre to watch "The Passion of the Christ." I remember leaving with my wife, and literally being unable to even talk about what we had just witnessed. The brutality was overwhelming. It remains today the most violent film I have ever seen. There was a time, years ago, when I tried to watch it on every Good Friday. It became impossible.

And now here I stood.

"Realize," Anton told us, "this would have been Caiaphas' palace. Take a moment, and we will head back up."

Not a word was spoken among us. It was strange; I did not feel like praying. What I really wanted to do was scream, just to let everything out, the pain I felt. It was "The Passion of the Christ" staring me in the face.

And then we went into Judgement Hall, and the question that had always bothered me.

> "Now at the feast the governor was accustomed to release for the crowd any one prisoner whom they wanted. And they had then a notorious prisoner, called Barab'bas. So when they had gathered, Pilate said to them, "Whom do you want me to release for you, Barabbas or Jesus who is called Christ?"

Jesus would have stood in this room, Pontius Pilate between him and the murderer, Barabbas.

And this is where I had always struggled. This was the easiest decision of all time. Release a man who had formed a huge following, who they had seen performing miracles of all kinds, who they had seen preaching for the poor and describing the Kingdom of God, or release a murderer? I had seen every Hollywood production, Jesus, Barabbas and Pilate standing on a stage outside in the daylight, crowds chanting over a fence for both men, the chants of "free Barabbas" drowning out those of Jesus, and then the horrific screams of "Crucify him!" "Crucify him!."

I have watched the scene hundreds of times. And I never understood why. The Walking Encyclopedia had the answer.

"Look at this room," he told us.

It was long, deep and rectangular in shape.

"It was a rigged game," Anton said. "A stacked deck. They likely brought Jesus here at night. His many followers were not even aware he had been arrested. The people here were not the same people who shouted "Hosanna to the Son of David" as Jesus rode into their city on a donkey on Palm Sunday. These were Judeans, and they were following the religious leaders. And those leaders wanted Jesus killed."

And now it made sense. A night time scene in a room where they packed the front with locals who did the bidding of the religious leaders. Those religious leaders would have worked the room in advance. Jesus' followers would have been shuffled to the rear. It may well have been the middle of the night when Pilate asked the crowd to choose. Jesus never had a chance.

> *".....But the chief priests stirred up the crowd, so that he should rather release Barabbas to them. Pilate answered and said to them again, "What then do you want me to do with Him whom you call the King of the Jews?" So they cried out again, "Crucify Him!" Then Pilate said to them, "Why, what evil has He done?" But they cried out all the more, "Crucify Him!" So Pilate, wanting to gratify the crowd, released Barabbas to them; and he delivered Jesus, after he had scourged Him, to be crucified....."*

"Also remember," Anton told us, "that Jews wanted someone to overthrow the Romans. Jesus' message was peace, and turning the other cheek. Barabbas may have been a popular fighter to the crowd, one of their own arrested for violence. Perhaps the Jewish crowd thought he was more likely to help them overthrow Rome than Jesus was."

I looked around at the others in our group. Many were nodding. I wondered if they had the same question answered that had long bothered me. Once again, the Walking Encyclopedia came through.

People did not choose Barabbas that day: they rejected Jesus. Remember, Jesus also died for Pilate, for the Pharisees, and for those in the crowd chanting "crucify him!" There is no record as to what became of Barabbas. He is insignificant in the future of mankind. But the record of Jesus, the one they chose to crucify on the cross, is the most significant in the history of mankind.

We left and made our way back to the bus. I learned things today. But I also felt pain. But it was nothing compared to what was about to come.

The cross was awaiting me.

"Then the soldiers of the governor took Jesus inside the praetorium and gathered the whole cohort around him. They stripped off his clothes and threw a scarlet military cloak about him. Weaving a crown out of thorns, they placed it on his head, and a reed in his right hand. And kneeling before him, they mocked him, saying, "Hail, King of the Jews! They spat upon him and took the reed and kept striking him on the head. And when they had mocked him, they stripped him of the cloak, dressed him in his own clothes, and led him off to crucify him."

CHAPTER 31

The Way of the Cross

"As the soldiers led him away, they seized Simon from Cyrene, who was on his way in from the country, and put the cross on him and made him carry it behind Jesus."

"Station Seven"

As our bus returned to the hotel in near darkness, Ayob stood up to address us.

"I know you are all very tired," he said. "But the wakeup call is 6am tomorrow."

The Way of the Cross

There was a moan throughout the bus.

"It will be hot and crowded. Wear your best walking shoes," he smiled. "We are walking with Jesus."

I knew we were near the end of our journey. The shoes could only mean one thing. It was really about to happen. We were walking with the cross tomorrow, up the hill, to Golgotha.

"Get some sleep," Ayob said as we departed the bus.

Sleep? Before this walk? That would be impossible.

I sat in my room and looked out into the darkness of Jerusalem. A bustling city, packed with tourists, had turned quiet in the late night hour. I turned on a light, sat in a chair, and opened my small Bible. It's one thing to know the story. Now, I was about to live it. And then I woke up, in the chair, the Bible clenched tightly in my hands.

The bus ride was quiet. It was as if everyone was preparing themselves for this day. What we weren't prepared for was the crowd when the bus stopped. There were people everywhere. It was all anyone could do just to walk. There were tourists and street sellers, beggars and tour guides. Small cars honked their horns weaving their way inch by inch through the crowd past us.

"Just find your way back to bus 92," Ayob hollered as we left. "Good luck!"

And then we were on our own, scattered in a maze of people.

They call the Way of the Cross the Via Dolorosa. It is Latin, meaning "The Way of Suffering." The road was paved with original stones from Jesus' time. The path was about a half mile long. It is not really one street, but a route of several streets, marked off by 14 different stations, 9 outside, and the final five inside the Church of the Holy Sepulcher, the final resting spot of the cross.

I spotted Anton in the crowd and got as close as I could to hear him hollering.

"This is the actual path where Jesus carried the cross," he was telling a group. "But where he walked has been buried by time far below where we are today."

And then I heard people calling for the walk to begin. I looked behind me, and saw the cross, with people all around it. A moment frozen in time. I made my way to where they were near the beginning, where Pontius Pilate's palace was. I looked up and again heard Anton above a huge crowd.

Destination: Holy Land

"We are at the intersection of Via Dolorosa and Al-Wa," he hollered. "This is the street that divides the Christian and Muslim communities."

And then the huge cross began moving. One person carrying from the front, another from the back, one more on each side. You could not get near the cross, as hundreds swallowed it up. People were chanting prayers and singing. Street sellers were hawking tee shirts and souvenirs.

If I had hoped for a quiet, serene place of prayer with the cross, I was in the wrong place.

The stations were marked by Roman numerals, etched in brass medallions. At each station are biblical accounts of what happened at that exact spot. We left the first station, where Jesus was condemned to death, and began the slow journey up the hill. At the second stop, where Jesus took up the cross, I watched as everyone carrying the cross handed it over to a new group of four that jumped on. I thought back to the St. Anne Church, where I had the chance to sing, but waited too long. I knew at that moment it would haunt me.

I would not let it happen again. I would carry the cross, just like I carried it in my dreams, when I woke up holding my Bible.

The third stop on the journey is where Jesus fell for the first time. I see the sign and I feel the heartbreak. I picture the mocking and insults from the crowd that day. The cross keeps moving and I know what is coming next. Jesus will see Mary at the fourth station. I close my eyes and picture what the moment was like, both for the son and the mother.

The cross is being passed back and forth again, as I try to make my way closer. I see people in front of me at the fifth station, standing by a wall. I head that way and find an ancient church with an old stone next to the church door. There was a sign there that said "where he stumbled and left his palm print indented." People were putting their palms in the same spot. The handprint of Jesus? Sign me up.

Then the cross passed station five, where Simon of Cyrene helped Jesus carry the cross. More people were leaving and joining the cross. As we came to station six, where Veronica wiped the face of Jesus, I searched the crowd for anyone from our group. I could not find anyone. There were just too many people. It was too loud. The cross was moving too quickly. I kept pushing my way closer. The cross was heading up the hill. I heard someone holler, "station seven!" Those carrying the cross from station six turned to hand it off.

To me.

The Way of the Cross

And time stood still again. I know my feet were moving. I know my ears were hearing. But I could not feel either of them. I was carrying Jesus' cross, the left arm, up the hill, to Golgotha, my eyes closed, trying to put myself in his footsteps for a few short moments.

I had already stood where Mary met Gabriel, fell to my knees where Jesus was born in the manger, knelt in the Sea of Galilee, and prayed in the Garden of Gethsemane. And now, here I was, carrying the cross to Calvary. There simply are no words.

And I did what I always do. I began singing to myself.

> "......You stood before my failure
> And carried the cross for my shame
> My sin weighed upon Your shoulders
> My soul now to stand......"

We reached the seventh station, where Jesus would fall for the second time. I knew it was time for me to let go now, to share the cross experience with those behind me. I closed my eyes one last time, then turned around to hand it off.

And standing right there beside me were Gene Couri and Delores Kouri. I looked at Gene, a man I respected dearly, who had a twinkle in his eye as I handed him the cross. He was holding onto Delores, the young at heart lady pushing 90 who probably weighed less than that. It was hot now. The path up the hill was steep. And I remembered what Delores told me earlier in the trip.

"This is the highlight of my life. I am not sure how I am going to handle all of this. What a thrill. I am so glad I am here for this."

Where Gene had a twinkle, Delores was no nonsense, staring straight ahead, as she put her arms around the cross. I know what it meant to me. I could only imagine what it meant to her.

I followed them to the eighth stage, where Jesus met the women of Jerusalem, where they handed the cross off to people behind them. I nodded at Gene. Delores smiled and gave me a thumbs up. I thought to myself, "this is so cool."

We walked forward to the ninth stage, where Jesus would fall for the third time. And then the Holy Sepulchre was in front of us.

As we prepared to enter, a man turned and asked me a question.

"On a scale from one to ten......"

I laughed, and he laughed back.

"Better bring out those Roman numerals," I said.

And then we walked into the holiest site on earth.

> *"....So what can I say?*
> *And what can I do?*
> *But offer this heart, Oh God*
> *Completely to you...."*

What a day.

> *"A large number of people followed him, including women who mourned and wailed for him. Jesus turned and said to them, "Daughters of Jerusalem, do not weep for me; weep for yourselves and for your children. For the time will come when you will say, 'Blessed are the childless women, the wombs that never bore and the breasts that never nursed! Then "'they will say to the mountains, "Fall on us!" and to the hills, "Cover us!"' For if people do these things when the tree is green, what will happen when it is dry?"*

CHAPTER 32

The Holy Sepulcher

"They brought Jesus to the place called Golgotha (which means "the place of the skull"). Then they offered him wine mixed with myrrh, but he did not take it. And they crucified him. Dividing up his clothes, they cast lots to see what each would get. It was nine in the morning when they crucified him. The written notice of the charge against him read: the king of the jews."

"Were you there when they crucified my Lord?"

Destination: Holy Land

The first thing you notice as you approach the Holy Sepulcher are the wooden front doors.

"These are the original doors," Anton told our group as we gathered at the front. "They are over 2,000 years old."

And on cue, everyone is touching the doors. Me included.

The second thing you notice once you venture inside, this site, the holiest site on earth for Christians, the most visited site in Jerusalem's Old City.......felt like a run down shopping mall in the middle of New Orleans.

How do you explain awe and frustration at the same time?

This is where Jesus was crucified, buried, and rose from the dead. Everything was here for me. I came to pray, to find my quiet moments. But it quickly became difficult. The crowd was overflowing, and everything appeared disjointed. I pictured a holy sight, a solemn place where I could pray at the cross, and then the empty tomb. Instead I got thousands of people, surrounded by glitz and glitter. There was shouting from guards, and people taking selfies in front of the holy sites. Wait times in line went for hours. And hours. And hours.

Disneyland has nothing on the Holy Sepulcher. But it mattered little: you cannot possibly come to the Holy Land and not come here. But be aware.

After struggling to find my way through the building, I found a Franciscan priest sitting on a bench and asked him for a little advice. He smiled.

"Well, for starters, there are four different religious groups who own the church," he said. "And they all have four different ideas on what it should look like."

"Four?" I asked. "This is a Christian site. Why?"

The priest just shrugged his shoulders. I pointed out various renovations that were happening around us.

"They are always working on something, building something," he said. "It becomes impossible to walk through with the crowds. It is very frustrating to all of us."

The church was built in the 4th century. Just inside the front doors are the five remaining steps for the Way of the Cross, leading up to Calvary. I began to make my way, following the crowd, but soon realized there were no labels or maps. The flow through the church became impossible, and as the Franciscan priest had warned me, renovations were happening wherever I went.

The Holy Sepulcher

But considering this site is where Jesus was crucified, there was an empty tomb, he was buried and resurrected, well, I could put up with the flames of hell to see what still lies before me. I watched the walking mass go by me and started making my way further. I kept walking through dim areas with little light. Everywhere I looked, the building was in poor repair. It was not serene, it was gaudy, and there was certainly no wow factor, just a succession of small, dark rooms to wander through.

Fortunately, I encountered some walking mass services with organ music that filled my spirits. And as I slowly moved along, still finding the crowds and the disjointed patterns, I also realized that everything I was seeing had incredible details. They may have been wasted in a dilapidated building, but once there, before your eyes, they were phenomenal.

I stopped at the Stone of Anointing, believed to be the site where Jesus' body was prepared for burial by Joseph of Arimathea. I knelt and prayed, and watched others place personal items on the stone slab. I then moved onto what was called the Katholikon, the main worship area of the church. It was a huge space with large arches and chandeliers inside. I found a chapel dedicated to Mary Magdalene, and another to Adam, where it says his skull is buried. I kept walking and saw a large crowd gathered outside a window. A person next to me said it was the "immovable ladder," symbolizing the shared denominations of the church. Further ahead I came to the Rock of Calvary, with the crack going through it, the crack caused by the earthquake that followed Jesus' death.

Those sites were nice, but I was looking for Golgotha.

I kept walking and walking, through disjointed hallways, following people, searching for the cross. I found another priest sitting on a bench.

"Golgotha?" I inquired. "Calvary?"

He pointed to some steps.

"Upstairs. Second floor. Just look for the long line," he smiled.

I said thanks, and began to leave.

"It will be a very, very long line," he said.

"If it takes forever," I told him. "I will be the last man standing there."

"You might want to go to the bathroom first," he smiled.

That proved to be good advice. The line was forming before I got to the top of the steps. I stood and waited. Some people in front of me gave up and left. I didn't travel 6,000 miles to walk away from this. No chance.

I waited and read my small Bible. Time went by. And then I was there, above the cross, looking down.

Destination: Holy Land

"Two minutes!" a Muslim guard screamed at me.

There were two chapels with beautiful mosaics. One showed Jesus nailed to the cross. The other had Abraham binding Isaac. Breathtaking. There was a very large altar where people were praying and touching the rock where the crucifixion took place.

I bowed my head and closed my eyes.

> "..... Were you there when they crucified my Lord?
> Were you there when they crucified my Lord?
> Oh! Sometimes it causes me to tremble, tremble, tremble.
> Were you there when they crucified my Lord?....."

We were being moved along quickly. Hours in line for two minutes at the cross. A deal I would make every day. Those two minutes stay with me forever. And now there was one more thing for me to see: the empty tomb. To me, the reason to go to the Holy Land, and to venture to the Holy Sepulcher, is to see the empty tomb. I began walking, and my head kept ringing.

> "..... Were you there when they laid him in the tomb?
> Were you there when they laid him in the tomb?
> Oh! Sometimes it causes me to tremble, tremble, tremble.
> Were you there when they laid him in the tomb?....."

I found a large rotunda with two rooms inside, one of them holding the "Angel's Stone," believed to be one of the stone's concealing the tomb. A priest was at the entrance, letting three people in at a time. I entered with two elderly women, locked in my arms on each side. It was right now, my moment, standing at the empty tomb. No matter the crowd, the lines, the building, the renovations, the gaudy atmosphere, nothing would not take these minutes away from me.

I helped the ladies kneel down and then knelt beside them and prayed.

> "....Were you there when they rolled the stone away?
> Were you there when they rolled the stone away?
> Oh, Sometimes it causes me to tremble, tremble, tremble,
> Were you there when they rolled the stone away?....."

I helped them get up to leave. I was composed, amazingly. They both had tears in their eyes.

"Thank you," they both said.

Unable to talk, I just nodded.

The Holy Sepulcher

I somehow made my way back down to find our group, and bus number 92. Today I had carried the cross up to Calgary, and then walked inside the most holy site in the world, the center of my faith, where my Lord and Savior was crucified and buried. It is just hard to describe. My emotions were frayed.

There were friendly faces waiting for me. I remembered the quiet somber bus ride we had made earlier that morning, knowing what the day would bring. Now, bus 92 was exploding in exaltation. Everybody was talking at once about what the day had meant to them. I just listened, smiled, and took it all in. How wonderful to see so many people touched by their faith.

And then.......

"Bob!"

It was Delores Koury.

"Bob! We carried the cross!"

"We did," I smiled. "And did you see the cross here?"

She nodded, slowly.

"And the empty tomb?" I asked.

And she smiled. "I saw it."

I looked in her eyes. I knew her life was fulfilled today. So was mine.

"With a loud cry, Jesus breathed his last. The curtain of the temple was torn in two from top to bottom. And when the centurion, who stood there in front of Jesus, saw how he died, he said, "Surely this man was the Son of God!"

CHAPTER 33

Ascension Chapel

"When he had led them out to the vicinity of Bethany, he lifted up his hands and blessed them. While he was blessing them, he left them and was taken up into heaven. Then they worshiped him and returned to Jerusalem with great joy. And they stayed continually at the temple, praising God."

It was very late again when we arrived back to our rooms. No spaghetti, so I passed on dinner once again. My stomach may have been empty, but my heart was full. I again went to my window, looked out upon the darkness, and tried to comprehend everything that had happened to me that day. And then I reached for my headphones, found my music, and cranked up the volume.

> *"....Healed and forgiven*
> *Look where my chains are now*
> *Death has no hold on me*
> *'Cause Your grace holds that ground*
> *And Your grace holds me now...."*

All I could think about was carrying the cross up the hill. And then to hand it off to Gene and Delores. And then to see Jesus hanging from that cross at Golgotha. And then my two minutes, at the empty tomb, with those ladies, and seeing the tears running down their faces. And then the euphoria with everyone back on the bus, listening to them gloriously tell the stories of their day, the stories similar to mine.

Ascension Chapel

I knew I had to get some sleep. The garden, the cross, and the tomb were behind me now. There was exultation still ahead.

As usual, I opted for the watered down tang for breakfast. People asked me what I missed most while I was in the Holy Land and my answer was always orange juice. One of the morning chefs at the hotel, a man named Lavi, had heard of my eating habits, and would make me some scrambled eggs on the side of all the hummus breakfast dishes.

"No hummus today, Bob?" he would ask, with a smile, knowing very well the answer.

"Not today."

"I can make you fresh lemon garlic hummus. It is very good."

"No thanks."

"How about squash hummus?"

"Seems a little early for me."

"Dill pickle hummus?"

"Absolutely not."

"Sweet potato hummus?"

I paused.

"I will take that sweet potato, with a ribeye steak, medium well."

Lavi laughed.

"Enjoy your orange juice," he said with a grin.

I just laughed and shook my head.

Our bus headed out to Ascension chapel, sitting in an enclosed courtyard atop the highest place in the Mount of Olives. The first church here dates back to the 4th century. This is the spot where Jesus gathered his disciples and ascended into heaven after his resurrection. The small, dark chapel is combined with a mosque, as Muslims also consider it a holy site, celebrating the prophet Isa. The star attraction for Christians is a slab of stone, surrounded by candles, called Ascension Rock, that is believed to contain the right footprint of Jesus. It would have been the last point he touched on earth before his ascension into heaven.

If it indeed was Jesus' foot, it was much larger than my size 12.

I watched and listened as tourist after tourist came by, put their foot by the rock for comparison, and debated with each other whether or not that was really Jesus' footprint. Meanwhile, next to the rock was a donation box. Combined with the chapel being connected to a mosque, it just felt.......a little odd.

Destination: Holy Land

The moment of the Ascension is told in the Book of Acts, in one very simple sentence. "He was lifted up before their eyes in a cloud which took Him from their sight."

There are Arabic inscriptions inside the chapel. Outside were vendors hawking their souvenirs. Other than the alleged footprint of Jesus, there really was not much to see here. Our group left the church and began strolling the hillside, with Anton leading the way.

"Look out at the crest of the Mount," Anton told our group. "There is a little village over the mountains called E-Tur. They have a giant bell tower on top of a church. It is run by nuns. Over 100 years ago, the father of the church, a man named Parthenius, was found stabbed to death in his cell. The case was never solved."

Anton smiled. A cold case in the Holy Land. The Walking Encyclopedia strikes again.

Tour buses were arriving by the minute. The small chapel was about to be overrun. It dawned on me that this was the end of Jesus' earthly journey, and near the end of mine.

I stopped again and looked around. This area is where the first Christians would have gathered, likely in a cave lower down the Mount, fearful to be seen worshiping in public. Imagine what those meetings must have been like after what they had witnessed.

"Take some time for yourself," Anton told the group. "Meet back here in an hour."

I walked along Ruba-el Adawiya Street and came to the Ascencion Coffee Shop. I looked at the menu.

French Fries.

I walked to the counter.

"French fries, please"

"Do you want Shawarma with your fries?"

"Not today, thank you."

"Large or small fries?"

"Definitely large"

"Would you like amba mango sauce with the fries?"

"No thank you," I smiled, as if I knew what that was.

I sat down, considered it a victory that I found french fries in the Mount of Olives, and looked out at the world in front of me. I knew Gethsamane was to my west; the Pater Noster Church to my south; As I left the cafe I found a beautiful lookout point, where I could see much of Jerusalem

Ascension Chapel

below. I noticed other churches nearby, one Greek and one Russian. A Muslim Hospital was across the street.

I walked along the beautiful landscape around me and thought what that day must have been like for the disciples, to be with Jesus on that mountain. If there was shock when he appeared to them on Sunday in the upper room, there had to be absolute glorious celebration to be with him again in that cave. Everything they had thought they lost, was now in front of them, and with it, the gift of eternal life.

I close my eyes and I picture the greatest party of all time. And I hear Jesus giving them their marching orders.

"Go and make disciples of all nations, baptizing them in the name of the Father, and of the Son and of the Holy Spirit, and teaching them to obey everything I have commanded you. And surely I am with you always, to the very end of the age."

And the disciples listened. And they went.

I headed back toward the chapel, where I saw a priest standing by the front door.

"Hello," I said. "My name is Bob. I am writing about the Holy Land."

He smiled and we shook hands.

"Father Faltas," he said. "Ibrahim Faltas. And I just finished writing a book."

"Really?" I said.

"Yes, it is about the work of the Franciscans in Bethlehem."

I asked him about being a priest at such a holy place, and learned that he has lived his whole life in Jerusalem. I told him I found it odd that such a holy Christian place was in a mosque. He nodded.

"But people of all faiths come here from everywhere."

We paused and I asked what life was like for people living in the area.

"Few people can pay rent in Jerusalem. It is difficult here, more so than in America."

I mentioned the number of Christians dwindling in the Holy Land.

"We must maintain the Christian presence here," he said. "We need to help people stay in the Holy Land, to be disciples."

My time was up. I thanked Father Faltas and began to leave, knowing that I needed to be that disciple, in some way, in my own life. It would start by putting a pencil to a piece of paper, and telling of my journey.

We got back at the hotel with a free afternoon. Lavi was ready for me.

"Mr. Bob, hummus for lunch?"

"Cheeseburgers?" I inquired.

And we laughed.

Tomorrow would be our final day in the Holy Land. The group would be visiting the Dead Sea, where you could swim and never sink, thanks to the salt water. Some talked about staying back, and making their own journeys somewhere around Jerusalem. There was talk of going back to Gethsemane, or the Wailing Wall. For me, there was one more thing to see. It wasn't on the itinerary, and I had no idea if it still existed.

But I was going to try.

"After the Lord Jesus had spoken to them, he was taken up into heaven and he sat at the right hand of God. Then the disciples went out and preached everywhere, and the Lord worked with them and confirmed his word by the signs that accompanied it."

CHAPTER 34

The Road to Emmaus

"Now that same day two of them were going to a village called Emmaus, about seven miles[a] from Jerusalem. They were talking with each other about everything that had happened. As they talked and discussed these things with each other, Jesus himself came up and walked along with them; but they were kept from recognizing him."

This is the story of how I had brownies and ice cream for breakfast.

I knew the hotel had arranged for drivers to take their guests to different locations. I just did not know if mine even existed.

"The Road to Emmaus," I told the hotel clerk. "Does it exist? Can a driver get me there?"

The clerk did not know but made a phone call. And then……

"My driver Uri says he will take you. He will be out front in 10 minutes."

I was going to Emmaus, wherever it was.

With gas at $7 a gallon, the streets of Jerusalem are dotted by tiny white cars. I managed to fit in, told Uri to head to the gas station, and pulled out my credit card.

"How far away is it?" I asked, fearing the worst.

"About 10 American miles," Uri said.

We chatted about his life in Jerusalem, and mine in America. My eating situation brought a smile to his face.

"Hold on," he said as we made a quick exit off Highway 1.

"Where are we?" I asked.

"Abu Ghosh," he said. "Your road is just ahead. But I have a surprise for you first."

We pulled in front of a small store. I could not tell if it was written in Yiddish or Hebrew. All I could make out was "Kho Bez."

"You hungry?" Uri asked.

"Starving, but……"

"Come on," he smiled.

And we walked into a bakery that smelled wonderful. I never found a Boston Cream or a Long John, but I found plenty. Uri called two men over and made them aware of my plight.

"Welcome," the first one said. "My name is Abu Ali. And this is Ahmed. What do you like?"

I paused and said "just about everything, I think…."

"Here," Ahmed said, pushing some colored balls in front of me. "Try these."

"What are they?" I asked.

"They are called Labneh balls," he said.

"I don't think so," I answered.

And they kept shoving treats in front of me.

"Any doughnuts?" I asked.

Abu Ali and Ahmed looked at each other.

"Wait here," Ahmed said.

A minute later he came back with a plate of brownies and a bowl of ice cream.

"Sold!" I said as I heard Uri laugh.

And within seconds, the brownies and ice cream made a successful landing.

Uri and I got back in the car.

"So there really is a road to Emmaus ?" I asked Uri.

"A beautiful road," he said.

We pulled into an area called the Ayalon Canada Park, and then walked into the Saxum Visitors Center. And then I was amazed.

Before me was an ultra modern, interactive mini museum, covering everything from Abraham to Jesus, with a 360 degree movie screen and come to life stories of Jesus' journey. I began taking notes when Uri brought a woman over to me.

"Hello," she said. "I am Isabel from the Center. Welcome to Saxum."

"This is phenomenal," I told her. "I would stay all day if Uri would let me. But….."

"But you came for the road?" she smiled.

"I did," I said. "As great as this is, I just want to stand on that old dirt road for five minutes."

"We have more than a dirt road," she told me as we walked over to a window and looked out the landscape below.

"The exact whereabouts of the road are a mystery," Isabel began. "We know it was small, and went through the hills of the Judean Mountains. It was likely on the way to Jaffa."

I was listening, but Isabel knew what I wanted.

"Follow me," she said.

We walked outside and Isabel stopped.

"Here we are."

I looked at a long trail that stood before me.

"It is about a twelve mile hike," Isabel said. "But I hope you brought water, because there are no water stations. There are four legs to the trail, and you can probably make the hike and then hike back in about five hours."

"Well, actually……"

Isabel smiled.

"I would love to," I said, "but Uri can't stay that long, can you Uri?"

I looked his way with wide eyes and pleaded.

"I see," Isabel said. "Why don't Uri and I go back inside, and give you a few minutes alone out here, and you can wander around a bit."

"That would be great," I said as I thanked her.

I looked at Uri.

"Meet me at the car in 15 minutes," I said.

And then I set foot on the trail, looking for my own quiet place. I found a large rock and sat down.

Only Luke tells us that Jesus appeared before two of his followers on the road to Emmaus after his resurrection on Sunday evening. Luke only named Cleopas, who is probably Cephas, and I always wondered how Luke could have one name, but not the other. Like many biblical stories, there are no answers. But I have always felt the second follower was Peter, because Luke tells us the men raced back to tell the other disciples. If it was not someone from their inner circle, how would they have known where to go, and why would the disciples have believed them?

Destination: Holy Land

No disciple was in more pain than Peter was, who had denied his Lord three times. No disciple needed more comforting. I sat on that rock, looked out on the road, and believed with all my heart that Jesus took the pain away from Peter at the moment.

Time stood still again. I watched as others looked around, some of them about to make that five hour hike down the Emmaus path.

"Make sure you have water!" I hollered as an elderly couple began hiking. They waved their bottles and smiled.

It was time to go. I got up to leave, and had a tremendous feeling that now I had seen everything I needed to see in the Holy Land. It was time to go home.

Uri was waiting for me.

"Well?" he asked.

"There really is a road to Emmaus," I told him. "And thanks for being so busy that you could not stay for me to make that 12 mile hike."

He laughed and we headed back. On the way we passed a McDonald's, and he looked at me.

I shook my head no.

"I should have met you a week ago," I told him.

We made small talk and he asked where I was from.

"Illinois," I said. "The Land of Lincoln. Abraham Lincoln was a famous American President."

"More famous than Trump?" he asked.

All I could do was wince and shake my head.

"Illinois?" he said. "I have another surprise for you. Just a slight detour."

We passed by a place called Chicken Broasted.

"No more food," I said. "I am fine."

"This is not food," Uri said. "There is someone you need to meet."

We drove for a few more minutes and pulled into a place called Mis'adat Abu Ghosh. It was another restaurant.

"Uri...." I began.

"Follow me," he said and we walked inside.

"Is Jawdat here?" he asked a woman behind the counter.

She hollered at the man who was setting up tables. He came over and said hello.

"This is Bob," Uri told him. "He is writing a book on the Holy Land, and he is from Illinois."

Jawdat smiled. "Illinois?" he said. "I used to live in Chicago."

"Tell him," Uri said.

I looked at Jawdat.

"I grew up here, went to America when I was 21, and lived in Chicago for six years. I was a tow truck driver."

"Go on," Uri said. "Tell him!"

Jawdat paused. "And then I won the lottery and came back home."

I just stared at him.

"Seventeen million dollars," he said, of course with a smile. "I could have gone anywhere. I chose to come back home, and try to make a difference, hoping to find a way for people of different faiths to get along."

I was stunned. My trip began in Haifa where I was searching for the same thing that Jawdat was seeking in Abu Ghosh. I told him about my journey.

"Here, we are 98% Muslim. But Jews and Christians know they are welcome here, and they come."

Jawdat, the richest and most famous man in town, spends his money trying to create opportunities for people of different faiths to come together. This is, when he is not waiting on tables in his restaurant.

We shook hands and said goodbye.

Back in the car, I looked at Uri.

"Any more surprises? I asked.

And he laughed. My road to Emmaus took some wonderful turns, and incredibly, ended like it began in Haifa.

"Then their eyes were opened and they recognized him, and he disappeared from their sight. They asked each other, "Were not our hearts burning within us while he talked with us on the road and opened the Scriptures to us?" They got up and returned at once to Jerusalem. There they found the Eleven and those with them, assembled together and saying, "It is true! The Lord has risen and has appeared to Simon."

CHAPTER 35

Ben Guiron

"Aggie, Gene, Gretta, Lolly, Delores, Ilda, Diana, Tony, Marybeth, and Bob"

About a half hour outside of Jerusalem is the Ben Guiron Airport, known far and wide for its security, which I would soon discover. Ben Guiron was the site of the famed 1972 attack by the Japanese Red Army killing 26 people, and injuring another 80 after firing machine guns into the passenger arrival area.

Armed guards check all vehicles entering the airport grounds. After we got dropped off, more guards were standing at the airport doors. Inside the airport were more armed guards, walking through the terminals. I watched as random people were being stopped and questioned.

We checked our bags, and were pointed toward a long check in line where guards were checking passports and boarding passes. Then onto another line to go through metal detectors. More guards, now asking questions. Why was I leaving Jerusalem? Why was I there? Had I been to any Arab countries while I was there?

I found it odd that there was little security coming into Tel Aviv, but it was in your face heading out.

I watched as passengers before me stepped into the metal detectors, surrounded by guards. It appeared they were doing random checks of passengers, making them disrobe some clothing. Fortunately for me, I was only wearing gym shorts and a tee shirt.

I stepped into the detector.

"Shirt off!" I heard a guard say.

"Who? Me?"

"Shirt off!"

I pulled the shirt over my head.

"Shorts down!"

Seriously?

"Shorts down!"

I pushed them down. I was now standing, barefoot, shirtless, shorts down to my knees, left only with my underwear, inside a metal detector with a guard staring at me. And then came the pat down.

I kept thinking about that movie "Midnight Express."

"You dress! Go!"

I was a free man. I pulled my clothes on, walked out of the metal detector, and saw the group of Couri's waiting for me with their mouths open.

"Bob!"

"Yeah, Bob the terrorist!"

"Be glad you didn't have the woman guard!"

Sometimes all you can do is laugh.

We passed a smoking lounge, a site no longer seen in America. A man walking next to me said the airport had banned them earlier, but people just started smoking in the bathrooms. As we neared our gate, the McDonald's cafe was waiting for us. I thought about it, then saw a sign that said the McRoyal combo was $16 American dollars. A few steps further and we came to the Burger King cafe. A double whopper meal could be had for $19.

Destination: Holy Land

I thought back to gas at $7 a gallon. It was definitely time to head back home.

This would be another overnight trip on the United Dreamliner. We took off, the pilot dimmed the overhead lights, and I looked around as people tried to sleep.

Not me. I pulled out my notebook. There was a journal to be written, no, a book, to be left for my children and grandchildren long after I was gone. Everything I had seen and done.

We were over the Mediterranean now, and I began going over all that had happened to me. My notes began with Safiya and Amir, playing tic tac toe. I went over my notes from Haifa, in that tiny and wonderful Wadi Nisnas neighborhood, where human beings of different cultures proved they could get along. I stared at what Anton had told me: "In Haifa, nobody looks at the color of your eyes."

I went through my notes on the Wailing Wall. I had capitalized all the different Jewish sects that were there, for hours, crying and praying. It was an impressive show of faith, even if it was different than mine. I turned the page and saw I was now in Beit Sahour, where I met Bassam and Hiyam, parents of my co-worker Sada. I smiled thinking about the book Bassam gave me, written in Arabic. I remember them crying asking about their daughter.

The in flight airplane map showed we were over Athens now. I kept flipping pages, looking at my notes, and remembering. I was praying where Gabriel came to Mary, and then to where Mary visited Elizabeth. And then to Bethlehem, where I found the city of my dreams to be in disrepair, taken over by Muslims. But there was still a Shepherd's Field there, where I knelt down, and a manger scene. I did not need notes for that. I closed my eyes and remembered the man I held hands with, two strangers, who had two minutes together under that curtain. How would I ever put that into words?

I turned the page and remembered the woman dancing at the Milk Grotto, hoping to become pregnant. And then we were off to the Jordan River, where I had hoped to get baptized, but sadly the river was not cooperating. I kept turning pages and reading. The Mount of Temptation, and then the Sea of Galilee. I paused. The Fishers of Men. Kneeling in the water. Beyond anything I could possibly imagine.

I put my notes down. We were over Spain now, about to leave the land below and hit the Atlantic. The plane was dark, except for the quiet hummings of the engines. It was the middle of the night now. I thought I would try to sleep.

No chance.

The notebook came back out, and I found myself in Cana, where water was turned to wine, and everyone was being married. And then St. Anne's Church. All I could do was shake my head and smile. Why didn't I get up on that altar and sing? That would be the regret of the trip.

The Sermon on the Mount, and then the archeology find in Mary Magdalene's town, Magdala. I stood on Mount Tabor where Jesus saw Moses, and then Capernaum and Bethany. And then, at the end, Jerusalem.

I paused again. I had to get some sleep.

"Good morning. Coffee or juice?"

I awoke to hear the stewardess coming toward me. My mind was groggy. Was I just swimming in the Sea of Galilee? And was it the security guard who made me disrobe swimming next to me?

"Juice, please," I said when she got to me.

I looked at the in-flight map. We were over New York now. Chicago was just down the road. I opened my notebook back up.

The young girl with the machine gun at the bus stop. The Last Supper room. And then it all hit me, and quick. I did not even need notes. Praying in the Garden of Gethsemane. Carrying the cross up to Calvary. The Holy Sepulcher. The cross. The empty tomb. The road to Emmaus.

I knew, if needed, I could talk for hours and hours about each site. The question was, could I write it to be left behind?

And then we landed.

AMEN

I finished the last chapter and turned on the television. Israel had just retaliated and killed the Hamas leader. This after war had broken out with Hezbollah, and Iran had launched attacks.

I thought about the Wadi Nisnas neighborhood in Haifa, and about Jawdat in Abu Ghosh. People trying their best to help everyone get along, and then watching this.

And I thought about Jesus, our Prince of Peace.

"If your enemy is hungry, feed him; if he is thirsty, give him something to drink."

"Make every effort to live in peace with everyone and to be holy; without holiness no one will see the Lord."

"In the world you will have tribulation. But take heart; I have overcome the world."

"You will go out in joy and be led forth in peace; the mountains and hills will burst into song before you, and all the trees of the field will clap their hands."

"Blessed are the peacemakers, for they shall be called sons of God."

"May the God of hope fill you with all joy and peace as you trust in him, so that you may overflow with hope by the power of the Holy Spirit."

Amen.

www.ingramcontent.com/pod-product-compliance
Lightning Source LLC
Chambersburg PA
CBHW050804160426
43192CB00010B/1639